FREEDOM

FROM FINANCIAL FEAR

FREEDOM

FROM FINANCIAL FEAR

D. James Kennedy, Ph.D.

Edited by Karen L. Gushta, Ph.D.

CORAL RIDGE
MINISTRIES

Fort Lauderdale, Florida

FREEDOM FROM FINANCIAL FEAR
By D. James Kennedy, Ph.D.

All Scripture quotations, unless otherwise indicated, are taken from the New King James Version. Copyright © 1982 by Thomas Nelson, Inc. Used by permission. All rights reserved.

Scripture quotation marked ESV is from The Holy Bible, English Standard Version®, copyright © 2001 by Crossway Bibles, a publishing ministry of Good News Publishers. Used by permission. All rights reserved.

ISBN: 978-1-929626-62-5

Cover and Interior Design: Roark Creative, www.roarkcreative.com

Published by Coral Ridge Ministries.
Printed in the United States of America.

Coral Ridge Ministries
P.O. Box 1920
Fort Lauderdale, FL 33302
1-800-988-7884
letters@coralridge.org
www.coralridge.org

CONTENTS

INTRODUCTION

It was an annual event—although the date might vary, it was never missed. Sometime in late October or early November, a Sunday was designated as "Stewardship Sunday." On this day Dr. D. James Kennedy would address the topic of giving. He wouldn't revisit it again until the next Stewardship Sunday. Anyone who skipped that service could safely attend Coral Ridge Presbyterian Church for the coming year without fear of being asked to "give." On the other hand, if you did attend the service, you were guaranteed to hear the subject covered with a cogency rarely matched.

The chapters in this book were drawn from the collection of stewardship sermons preached by Dr. Kennedy between 1978 and 2004. During this period there were times when the economy was in a downturn and times when our country was prospering. Yet these messages all share the same common themes: "You can't outgive God." "Giving is a matter of faith, not finances," and "God's promises never fail!"

In the 1978 sermon "On Giving and Receiving," Dr. Kennedy laid out the benefits of bountiful giving. In "Fully Persuaded," preached in 1980, he showed that our giving glorifies God. The

1984 sermon, "The Biblical Way to Financial Success" explains how to achieve the very essence of the Christian life—sufficiency in all things. The 1991 sermon, "Taking the Strain Out of Finances," shows us what life's greatest lesson is. In his 1993 sermon, "Open the Windows of Heaven," Dr. Kennedy expounded Malachi 3:10, and the 1995 sermon, "The Consecrated Thing," lists five key principles of Christian stewardship. The 1996 sermon, "Standing on the Promises," is a masterful exposition of the topic of God's promises, in general, and His promise concerning the tithe, in particular. The final sermon, preached in 2004, has the intriguing title, "Whatever Happened to That Widow?" In it Dr. Kennedy included many of his favorite examples of people who had learned life's greatest lesson and who saw great success as a result.

The biblical wisdom contained in these sermons is profound. Yet that is not their sole significance. Although Dr. Kennedy acknowledged that he never enjoyed preaching on this topic, he was himself "a sermon in shoes." In his biography, *D. James Kennedy, The Man and His Ministry*,[1] Herbert Lee Williams includes the following section describing Dr. Kennedy's own practice of Christian stewardship:

> Challenged by the example of a Christian college president who was returning a larger percentage of his salary to the Lord each year, Jim began the same experiment. In his own words:
> I started increasing the portion of my church salary that I was giving back—to 30 percent, then 50 percent. God was still providing my needs, so I increased it to 75 percent, to 90 percent, to 100 percent, and He was still providing my needs. When I gave away 100 percent of my salary, I had more money left than I'd ever had before. So I decided to tithe the second time around—that is, to go to 110 percent—and the next year I had more money left than I had had the previous year. I eventually got what I was giving away up between 100-150 percent of my salary, and still the Lord was providing for my needs for five or six straight

years. So, we decided to up our giving to 200 percent. God simply gives me what I need in other ways.

This enabled Jim in 1998 to reach the long-sought goal of giving back to the church 100 percent of all of the salary he had earned at the church since he arrived in 1959. He did this to demonstrate the truthfulness of the promise of Malachi 3:10, where God says: "Bring ye all the tithes into the storehouse, that there may be meat in mine house, and prove me now herewith, saith the Lord of hosts, if I will not open you the windows of heaven, and pour you out a blessing, that there shall not be room enough to receive it." God has clearly stood behind this promise.

"So much for secular mathematics," says Jim. "God has His own higher mathematics, and you can't outgive Him."

In view of Dr. Kennedy's striking example, it's worth noting that only a small percentage of Christians in America appear to believe that "you can't outgive God." Although the Pew Forum on Religion and Public Life reported from a survey of 36,000 participants in 2007 that 76 percent of Americans identify themselves as "Christian" by faith, a survey by the Barna Group in the same year showed that just 5 percent of adults tithed.[2] According to George Barna, "a majority of the money donated by individuals in the U.S. comes from the *born again*[3] constituency." However, of the ninety-five million born again adults in America, only nine percent gave one tenth or more of their income. On the other hand, the Barna research found that 24 percent of *evangelical Christians*[4] tithed.

Today, many in our nation are fearful of the future. They wonder what will happen to their investments and how the next government intervention will affect them. There is good reason to be fearful. We are ignoring the biblical principles upon which our nation was founded—principles that have enabled us to achieve great success as a nation. Never has our country taken on as much debt—both personal and national—as we now have.

Never have we been as indebted to foreign creditors as we now are.

Congressman Todd Akin has noted, "Never have so many owed so much because of so few!" The more closely we look at what our leaders are doing in Washington, the more cause we have for alarm. Any one of a number of possible disaster scenarios could bring great devastation to our land.

Nevertheless, as great as our fears may be, our hope should be greater. As Dr. Kennedy stated in his sermon, "Standing on the Promises," although by nature we are promise breakers, God's promises never fail, and He has given us literally thousands of promises, all of which are "Yes!" and in Him, "Amen!" Some of these promises have conditions attached, however. Such is the case with God's promises to "open the windows of heaven" and to "rebuke the devourer." In order to receive the benefits of these promises, we must first fulfill God's condition.

While we may have little hope that the government will stop raising our taxes, or that we can find a surefire safe place to invest, we do know that God has promised never to leave us or forsake us. The context of this promise stated in Hebrews 13:5 surely applies: "Let your conduct be without covetousness; be content with such things as you have. For He Himself has said, 'I will never leave you nor forsake you.'" As Dr. Kennedy so forcefully taught, God's physical blessings upon us are not dependent upon what the government may or may not do. Instead, they are totally dependent upon whether we have learned life's greatest lesson, "Trust God!" So, today, with the government at our back, mountains of financial problems on each side, and a sea of endless debt in front of us, let us look up and profess that we will *trust God* for all that we need!

Karen L. Gushta, Ph.D.
Coral Ridge Ministries
Fort Lauderdale, Florida

Chapter One

ON GIVING AND RECEIVING

What's your attitude toward giving? Are you one of those who avoids attending church on "Stewardship Sunday," or have you learned to give "bountifully and cheerfully?" If you're like the ninety-one percent of born-again Christians who don't tithe, you may be surprised to learn that Dr. Kennedy agreed with the person who said, "Money is nothing to God except an index to our souls." In this chapter, you'll see why.

"But this I say: He who sows sparingly will also reap sparingly, and he who sows bountifully will also reap bountifully."
— 2 Corinthians 9:6

There was a pastor who had a very ingenious idea on Stewardship Sunday. He had all of the pews rigged with electrical wires. Then, while asking the congregation how many would tithe, he pushed a button that sent a current through the wires. The whole congregation jumped up—but afterward they found three Scotsmen who had been electrocuted!

A Scotsman of a different kind was the great preacher, Dr. Alexander Whyte. He said something in a more serious vein about the same problem:

> Most men, it is to be feared, have no principle
> and no method in their giving. They dole out their

contributions and subscriptions as if it were a real intrusion and a cruel injury that they suffer just to be asked to give. Thus, they neither get the good, nor do the good that intelligent, conscientious, methodical giving always brings with it.

SOWING OR THROWING?

We are told not to give grudgingly or of compulsion or constraint, for God loves a cheerful giver. The problem is that some people wrestle with that, and they just can't give very cheerfully; it really hurts when they give! Maybe the problem is that they do not see it in a biblical sense. Our text says, "But this I say: He who sows sparingly will also reap sparingly, and he who sows bountifully will also reap bountifully" (2 Corinthians 9:6). Sadly, many people look on their giving not as *sowing*, but as *throwing*. They think that they are throwing it away, and thus it pains them, as was said of the man who put a nickel in the plate and then sang with might and main, "When we asunder part, it gives me inward pain."

The Bible says that we are not throwing; we are sowing. There are unalterable laws involved, and those who sow sparingly shall reap sparingly, and those who sow bountifully shall reap bountifully. Does the Bible indeed teach that God blesses us as we give to Him? Does the Bible teach that there is a receiving as well as a giving? Our text obviously makes that plain. The Scripture says that we should learn to develop a sense of altruism, that we should give for the needs of others, and that we should give out of love to God.

The Apostle Paul was a great giver because he was a great receiver. He could say, "Thanks *be* to God for His indescribable gift!" (2 Corinthians 9:15), and that gift brought forth from his lips a paean of praise. His stewardship followed hard in the tracks of his praise, and he gave all he had and all that he was. Paul knew there were laws at work that God had built into the universe. God will not be placed into the debt of any man—no one can outgive God. He who sows, reaps.

Those laws in the spiritual world, as in the physical world, are based upon faith. It is an act of faith in the law of the harvest that a farmer exercises every spring when he takes perfectly good corn that could be made into perfectly good bread to feed his family and throws it away into the dirt. He does that because he knows that he is not throwing it away; he is sowing it and he will reap a harvest. The Bible repeatedly makes reference to these laws, for when we obey God's ordinances, we will be blessed. Whoever draws near unto the Lord, the Lord will draw near unto him (James 4:8). Those who honor God, God will honor.

In Proverbs 3:3 comes the command, "Let not mercy and truth forsake you; Bind them around your neck, Write them on the tablet of your heart." We ask, "Why should I be merciful and why should I exercise truth?" The answer comes back in verse 4, "*And* so [you shall] find favor and high esteem in the sight of God and man."

SOWING BOUNTIFULLY

There was a man by the name of William who became a Christian and gave the tithe (ten percent of his income) to the Lord. Then he decided that he would give offerings as well, and he gave twenty percent, which he later increased to fifty percent. In all of this time, God continued to bless him. When his children were out of college, he increased his giving to one hundred percent of his income. His name was William Colgate. I am sure that of the millions of people today who brush their teeth with one of his products, only a microscopically small number have any appreciation of the relationship between his phenomenal success and his obedience to the law of sowing!

Another man who began to tithe and then increased his giving until he gave most of his income to the Lord was named Heinz. However, I am afraid that many who daily use the products he developed do not realize that part of his phenomenal success was due to the fact that Henry J. Heinz observed the law of sowing. Likewise, H. P. Crowell gave the majority of his income to the work of Jesus Christ. If you're not familiar with him, you may be more familiar with his company—the Quaker Oats Company. Or how about James L. Kraft, who gave tremendous portions of his income to the work of Jesus Christ and was once quoted as saying, "The only investment I ever made which has paid consistently increasing dividends is the money I have given to the Lord."

So when you brush your teeth with Colgate, when you put Heinz ketchup on your hamburger, when you place that slice of Kraft cheese on your sandwich, I hope you will remember that the lives of these men give testimony to the truthfulness of the promise of God, "He who sows bountifully will also reap bountifully" (2 Corinthians 9:6).

There are many more men and women—too many to mention here—who knew that they were not *throwing*, they were *sowing* and consequently, God was blessing them. Here are just a few more examples:

- Robert Laidlaw, the businessman from Australia, whose book *The Reason Why* has sold millions of copies, gave great portions of his income to the work of Jesus Christ.

- A farmer who began to tithe testified, "This year I began to tithe to the Lord, and all I can say is that fall is come and my farm has yielded a greater increase than the one to the west, the east, to the north or to the south of me. I cannot explain it. I can only testify to the truthfulness of it."

- The superintendent of a factory said that for a dozen years he had tithed and for each of those dozen years God had blessed him, and his income had risen.

- The trustee of a large city church told a large group of young people about the blessings of tithing and bringing the offerings to God. So convinced was he that God would fulfill His promise, he challenged any of them who had not tithed to begin to do so, promising that if a year later they were the poorer for it, he would make up the difference.

THE INDEX OF OUR SOULS

These people truly believed in the promises of God. Do you? God, of course, does not need our money. Someone has well said that money is nothing to God except as an index to our souls. How is the index of your soul today? When you make your decision about giving, which is one of the most important decisions of all, do you come in faith? Do you believe Jesus Christ, trust Him, and know that you cannot outgive Him? How do you really feel about giving to the Lord? If it hurts you to give, then you really believe that giving is self-impoverishment! If you believe God, then you know that giving is self-enrichment. You cannot outgive God!

On several occasions I have shared my own experience over the years. We increased from ten percent, on up and up, until a number of years ago we reached a hundred percent. Last year we gave over a hundred percent of my salary. I can only say to you that in every one of those years God increased my income and opened the windows of Heaven, so that I ended up with more than I would have had if I had kept it all. You cannot outgive God!

C.T. Studd was a famous British scholar, Cambridge graduate, outstanding athlete, and famed missionary. After graduating from Cambridge and having an outstanding career in British athletics, Studd decided to give it up to go to the mission field. He had inherited great wealth, but he also gave that up. During his lifetime he gave away over five million dollars to the cause of world missions. That was back in the time when five million dollars was an almost unheard-of sum. After he died, a small slip of paper was found on which he had scribbled these words that have had a great impact upon me—and I hope they will upon you. He said, "Gladly would I make the floor my bed, a box my chair, and use another box for my table rather than suffer men to perish eternally for want of knowledge of Jesus Christ." His motto was: "If Jesus Christ is God and died for me, then no sacrifice can be too great for me to make for Him."

C.T. made great sacrifices to serve Christ, yet what do we know about sacrificing for Jesus Christ? If money is the index of our souls, how does yours measure? How much are you really concerned over lost people? Do you really care? Recently we had an opportunity to begin a new ministry. Many people said they would like to be involved in it. Then I received a report that one after another individuals said, "Please, have me excused." It was a chance to reach people for Jesus Christ, but it would have cost them something. As I noticed one person after another cancel out, my heart was saddened. The problem in most cases was that the person was just not really concerned enough about other people. If the church of Jesus Christ had half the concern that C.T. Studd indicated in his note, the Great Commission of Jesus Christ would be fulfilled this year!

THE ONLY ANTIDOTE TO COVETOUSNESS

I once read of a priest who, after listening to the confessions of people for many, many years, made the observation that never in all of those decades had any person ever confessed the sin of covetousness! Does that mean that none of those people had ever coveted? No—I believe that example simply shows that covetousness is so insidious, so subtle, and so stealthy in the way it wraps itself around our hearts and souls and squeezes the love of God out of us that many people do not realize that it is there.

Jesus said, "Beware of covetousness" (Luke 12:15), and, of course, the only antidote for covetousness is giving. We can have every good purpose, every good intention, but it comes right down to the point where we must make the choice. What makes Jesus Christ so different from everyone else? All through His life He was faced with difficult choices—beginning with the temptation in the wilderness and culminating in the temptations in the Garden of Gethsemane and upon the Cross. His choice was whether He would save Himself or save others, and always, when it came to the hard choices of life, Jesus came down on the right side.

The problem today is that many in the church have good intentions. They want the mission enterprise of the church to be extended, and they want to reach out for Jesus Christ. However, when it comes to making the hard decisions—making the pledge, making the commitment, and giving the gift, they fail. Ultimately, I am sure it is a combination of a failure of faith and love. Faith believes the promises of God and that God is concerned for us and that we cannot outgive Him! Concern for other people—a love for God is what motivates us and drives us.

There is a couplet that puts it very well:

There was a man—some called him "mad."
The more he gave, the more he had.

I am sure the world would call that man "mad." How about you? Deep down in your heart, what do you really think about the man who gives bountifully? Is he foolish? Unwise? Uncircumspect? Or do you see him as a man who genuinely believes the promise, "He who sows bountifully will also reap bountifully"? Or the promise, "I will open the windows of heaven and pour out such a blessing that there will not be room enough to receive it"?

There are some who have not even reached the basic platform of Christian giving, which is the tithe. They have not even begun to give offerings beyond the tithe. They find themselves still under the condemnation of the law of God found in Malachi 3:8-9, which says, "Will a man rob God? Yet you have robbed Me! But you say, 'In what way have we robbed

17

You?' In tithes and offerings. You are cursed with a curse, for you have robbed Me, even this whole nation." I would urge you now—step up not only to the basic platform of God, but also to His promises for truth. Heed the words of the apostle Paul, "He who sows sparingly will also reap sparingly, and he who sows bountifully will also reap bountifully" (2 Corinthians 9:6).

I am often grieved as I listen to those who struggle to make ends meet. The problem is that they have never learned to open their hands and give as unto the Lord—to give with rejoicing, to give with believing, to give voluntarily, to give spontaneously, and to give eagerly unto God. For when we do, we're not throwing it away—we are sowing it.

There was a man—some called him "mad."
The more he gave, the more he had.

Chapter Two

FULLY PERSUADED

"If we are to see God's abundance in our lives, if we are to be used in a great way by God in this world, it is going to be on the basis of our faith in the promises of God."

Claims such as this one were commonplace with Dr. Kennedy. However, as you will see in this chapter, he always backed them up with scriptural truth and testimonial evidence. Meditating on the example of Abraham, who *"was strong in the faith,"* Dr. Kennedy shows how we, too, can become fully persuaded of God's promises—particularly those that concern stewardship!

"He staggered not at the promise of God through unbelief; but was strong in faith, giving glory to God; and being fully persuaded that, what he had promised, he was able also to perform."

—Romans 4:20-21, KJV

When we have come to the end of our lives—when all the pages of the calendar have fluttered past, when all the water has flowed under the bridge and over the dam—as we look back upon the years of our lives, if we are perceptive, we will detect that everything good that has come into our lives has been the result of our believing the promises of God. This is the secret of the Christian life. Sad it is that many people live their lives in the church for years and never even dimly grasp this truth. It is the essence of the Christian faith! The Word of God expressly declares that if we do not believe the promise God has given us concerning His Son, we make Him a liar. Salvation itself is believing the promise of God. "And this is the promise that He has promised us—eternal life" (1 John 2:25).

FAITH IN GOD'S PROMISES

Faith in the Bible is always reflexive. Saving faith means first resting our hopes of eternal life upon Jesus Christ and His cross, and then taking God at His Word concerning what He says about those who trust in His Son. For example, if I asked, "Do you know that you are going to heaven?" you might say, "Oh, yes, indeed." I would then ask, "Why?" And you'd reply, "Because I am trusting in Christ." I might further respond by saying, "What makes you think that anybody who trusts in Christ shall ever see the inside of paradise?"

Indeed, what makes us think so at all? It is only the promise of God. What is true concerning our salvation is equally true in every other phase of the Christian life. If we are to see God's abundance in our lives, if we are to be used in a great way by God in this world, it is going to be on the basis of our faith in the promises of God.

Abraham was "the friend of God." What a magnificent title! He was also known as the "father of the faithful." And faithful, indeed, he was, for he was full of faith. Our text says, "He staggered not at the promise of God through unbelief, but was strong in faith, giving glory to God; and being fully persuaded that, what he had promised, he was able also to perform" (Romans 4:20, 21). Question: Are you a spiritual "staggerer"? Abraham was not. He staggered not at the promises of God, but he was fully persuaded. Are you fully persuaded that what God has promised, He is able also to perform? How much more should we be fully persuaded than Abraham was? Indeed, in Abraham's day there were precious few promises that God had given to man on which he could base his confidence. But now four millennia have passed. Unnumbered years have come and gone—years filled with God's promises—promises that have been kept by our great Creator. How much more, therefore, is it incumbent upon us today to be fully persuaded that what He has promised, He is able also to perform?

GOD CANNOT LIE OR DECEIVE

My friends, as we all know, unbelief among the unbelieving and unregenerate of this world is a sin. The Scripture speaks of those who have an "evil heart of unbelief." If unbelief in the unregenerate is a sin, we need to keep in mind that feebleness of faith in a believer is also a sin and a fault. One day we as Christians will have to give an account for this. How will our consciences be able to answer the question, "Why have you doubted?" Will it be said of us by our Savior, "O you of little faith!"

There are evidently degrees of faith in different believers. There are some who are strong in faith—like Abraham. There are others who are feeble of faith—men and women of little faith. Such a feeble faith is an affront to God. However, the same reasons that would cause us to rest our faith in Christ and God to any degree are sufficient reasons to cause us to rest our confidence in Him fully and be fully persuaded about Him.

It is true that our confidence in any man should always be measured and should be given cautiously and with great circumspection. Mankind is weak and frail; we are liars and deceivers. God, on the other hand, is the omnipotent One who can do all things. He is not like man, nor can He lie. God is the God of all truth, and no lie can ever pass from His lips. Therefore, we should place our faith fully and confidently and totally in our God. To do anything less is a denigration of His character and an affront to His person.

Would you not be insulted if you gave your word or promise to someone, and they looked you square in the face and said, "I do not believe you"? Of course! We would become extremely indignant. However, think of it, that we, as sinful, weak, frail, depraved men, become indignant because someone challenged our word, the word of a mere man, prone to lie and deceive. Yet, God can neither lie nor deceive, and we, in our vanity and pride, refuse to rest our confidence in Him!

PROMISES CONCERNING STEWARDSHIP

Some of you may say, "Well, my faith is strong." Is it now? I am sure that for some of you that is true. But I am also sure that there are many others who demonstrate very convincingly the feebleness and frailty of their faith every time the offering plate is passed in church. Every time a pledge card is received in the mail, they begin to "stagger through unbelief" in the promises of God. God has made many marvelous promises, and it seems that in the area of stewardship, God wants to strengthen our faith, build us up, and make us strong, even as we come to trust Him right now for our lives. For example, Paul tells us, "My God shall supply all your need according to His riches in glory by Christ Jesus" (Philippians 4:19). What a magnificent promise this is! Do you believe it? Or do you stagger at it? If we believe it, then there is no reason for us to worry about this world's goods—none whatsoever! We may trust God's promise, go about our daily work, and know that He will supply all of our needs out of His riches in glory.

There is a second promise that goes even beyond that. We are told that God has said, "'Bring all the tithes into the storehouse, that there may be food in My house, and try Me now in this,' says the Lord of hosts, 'If I will not open for you the windows of heaven and pour out for you *such* blessing that *there will* not *be room* enough *to receive it'"* (Malachi 3:10). That is a promise of God. Do you stagger at that promise like a drunken man weaving down the street, or are you strong in faith, fully persuaded that what God has promised He is fully able to perform? I think of the person who said, "Yes, but does that mean *before* or *after* taxes?" This reminds me of the person who is going into the river where people are swimming and the question in his mind is, "Is it below the kneecap or above the kneecap?" While others are cavorting, exulting, and enjoying themselves, he is shivering in the shallows.

Another promise which goes beyond these is the promise we find in Mark 10, where Jesus says to us, "There is no one who has left house or brothers or sisters or father or mother or wife or children or lands, for My sake and the gospel's, who shall not receive a hundredfold now in this time. . . and in the age to come, eternal life" (Mark 10:29-30). In 2 Corinthians the Bible says that he who sows sparingly will reap sparingly and he who sows abundantly will reap abundantly. Over the years I have seen examples of this. Those who do just enough not to legally be thieves in the Kingdom of God; i.e., those who just barely give their tithe are those who do find their needs met and have some blessings. However, those who throw themselves into the depths of the river of God's promises are those who find that God blesses abundantly. Indeed, there are many needs today but, my friends, may I remind you that our God is not limited by inflation!

A MATTER OF FAITH, NOT FINANCES

Stewardship and the fulfillment of the promises of God is not a matter of our finances; it is a matter of faith. If we do not stagger at the promises of God, we will find that He will abundantly bless us—even as He says, "a hundredfold." Those to whom that promise was made had given very generously—the Bible mentions houses, and lands, and other gifts of sacrifice. I have seen over the years that those who have given sacrificially have been greatly blessed, and yet, they are the last ones in the world who would ever say that they have given sacrificially.

Mr. Stanley Tam shared a wonderful testimony of how God blessed his life in a tremendous way. We saw how this man turned his business over to God, made Him a half partner, then a major partner, and then total owner of his business. He began to give tremendous amounts of money to the Lord's work around the world. He gave, he said, five hundred thousand dollars a year, and then seven hundred, then eight hundred, a million, and then five million dollars a year to the work of Christ.

A member of our church told me that years ago he had decided to take God at His Word. He began to give generously to the Lord's work, way beyond the tithe, and God blessed him. Over the years, the blessing continued to grow until he came to the place where he was praying that God would enable him to give a hundred thousand dollars a year to the Lord's work. He said that he was amazed when he checked this year and found that he had given a hundred and forty thousand and yet made more money than he had ever made in his entire life. I have found this same kind of experience in my own life.

There are some who say, "Yes, but those are rich people." Yet Stanley Tam told how he had to go to his father to borrow money to get started in his business. These people were not rich when they began to take God at his word. The man I just mentioned in our church was making one hundred and twenty-five dollars a week when he received Christ. No, that is a "cop-out" for those who are afraid to take God at His Word—those who are afraid to dive into the river of faith and trust the promises of God. Actually, those who stagger around and talk about the rich do not know that the problem is the covetousness in their own hearts.

It is tragic that some of these people will hear testimony after testimony from those who have swum out into the depths and found that God has opened such windows of blessing upon them that they do not know what to do with all of the abundance that has come. They hear these testimonies, and yet they still wring their hands in unbelief. They insult God, because they are quite sure that in their case, at least, it will not work. But remember the words of Jesus, who said that there is *no man* who has given this or that or the other who will not, in this life, now receive an hundredfold and in the life to come—eternal life.

GLORIFYING GOD

As I contemplated this text, certain things impinged upon my consciousness that seemed to be of tremendous weight and of great importance. The chief end of man is to glorify God and to enjoy Him forever,[5] and yet the only way we can glorify God is by being strong in faith. This text says of Abraham that "he staggered not at the promise of God through unbelief; but was strong in faith, giving glory to God." It is in the strength of our faith that we glorify God. I do not care in what area of life it breaks out, faith is always and invariably from the same root and source. Strong faith is a faith that rests in the claims and lays hold of the promises of God. It is only through people of such faith that God does his mighty works and brings glory to Himself. Therefore, we who have feeble faith are not only an affront to God's character, we are dishonoring God in His world, because He can do no mighty deeds through us; therefore His name is not glorified.

Strong faith glorifies God because it treats God like God— as the Omnipotent One for whom nothing is too hard. It treats God as the God of all truth who cannot lie and who will bring all His promises to pass. Though at times our patience may be stretched, it is true that in due time, in God's own time, He will fulfill His promise, if we stagger not. Abraham did not look upon the circumstances around him, upon the evidences of his senses impinging upon his mind—the deadness of his own body and the deadness of Sara's womb—but rather he claimed the promise of God, and God made his seed as numerous as the stars of the heavens. May Abraham, indeed, be the father of you—another who is filled with faith.

Whence then comes such faith? Faith is a gift from God; it is also an act of man. God gives it, and we exercise it. It is through the Holy Spirit that faith comes. Therefore, we should *pray for faith*. We should pray that God would make us men and women and boys and girls of strong faith, fully persuaded that God is able to do that which He has promised. After praying for that faith, we should then *step out in faith* and believe God. We will then be astonished at what God can do through us!

Chapter Three

THE BIBLICAL WAY TO FINANCIAL SUCCESS

The previous chapter showed that to receive God's blessings, we must be fully persuaded of His promises. This is far from being a kind of "prosperity gospel," as you'll see in this chapter. Why should we desire financial success? The mature Christian, Dr. Kennedy points out, does not covet the things of this world, but rather delights in using his or her abundance for the advancement of the Kingdom of Jesus Christ. Having "sufficiency in all things" enables us to have abundance for good works, so that His name may be glorified!

"And God is able to make all grace abound toward you; that you, always having all sufficiency in all things, may have an abundance for every good work."
                                        — 2 Corinthians 9:8

"That you, always having all sufficiency in all things," is a phrase that puzzled many scholars, because here Paul picks up the Stoic ideal of what life should be—the ideal of total self-sufficiency. This was an ideal both of the Greek Stoics and Cynics. It has caused people to wonder, why would Paul place this in such an important verse where he is describing, in effect, the very essence of Christian life? Not only is it an ideal of the Stoics and Cynics of old, but it is certainly an ideal of modern secularists as well—to be totally independent—to be totally self-sufficient.

SUFFICIENCY IN ALL THINGS

The Greek word *autarkeia* means the perfect condition of life in which no aid or support is needed; a sufficiency of the necessities of life or, subjectively considered, a mind which is contented with its lot. It is related to the word *autarkēs* which means strong enough or possessing enough to need no aid or support from anyone, which is what most people in our world today are seeking—to be totally self-sufficient and totally independent. The question we must ask ourselves is, "How do we gain this complete self-sufficiency, this *autarkeia*?"

We become self-sufficient by *sowing bountifully*, by giving bountifully to the needs of God's people and God's Kingdom—above and beyond the tithe. The state of *autarkeia* does not come by self-seeking, by self-advancement, or by self-protection. It comes through an "hilarious," or cheerful and joyous service to God and to the people of God. Paul tells us, "God loves a cheerful giver" (2 Corinthians 9:7). The term "hilarious" is derived from the Greek word for "cheerful." Here Paul is telling us the secret to obtaining that which almost everyone today is trying to obtain—how to have all sufficiency, always, in all things. You will notice the abundance of terms he uses. The word "all" is repeated over and over again: "And God is able to make *all* grace abound toward you; that you, always having *all* sufficiency in *all* things, may have an abundance for every good work" (2 Corinthians 9:8). Here is a super abundance of all things by the grace of God.

TOTAL DEPENDENCE UPON GOD

I am sure that there are many people who are working toward self-sufficiency and complete independence in their lives, but Paul tells us that we can obtain it in a way that is much different than most people have ever imagined. He says, "He who sows sparingly will also reap sparingly, and he who sows bountifully will also reap bountifully" (2 Corinthians 9:6). In effect, Paul is saying that the way to complete self-sufficiency is by becoming independent from *men* and totally dependent upon *God* as the complete source of all of our needs.

A young minister once told me that he was very concerned about what he preached because of the attitude of some of his elders. He did not want to step on their toes, because he was afraid that this might affect his living and his salary. I said, "My friend, unless you come to the place where you are totally dependent upon God, you are going to be an utter failure in the ministry. If you begin to bend your message and clip the edges of it because you don't want to offend people and fear that your living will be diminished, you are no doubt on your way to becoming a complete failure as a minister." We should all feel utterly dependent upon God for our livelihood, for then we can act in our lives according to principle and not according to expediency.

THE "CULT OF PROSPERITY"

There are preachers in the land today who are always saying that you can get anything you want from God by giving to Him, and then He will bless you. They say that if you claim by faith in God whatever it is you want—whether it's a new Cadillac, a new boat, a new home, or whatever—and then give to Him, He will give to you. This "cult of prosperity," makes Christianity essentially man-centered, instead of God-centered. It's as though God exists in order to fulfill our desires and wants, and not the other way around. People act as though they have a little genie in a bottle that they can rub whenever they want something and God comes out. They pray, "Not thy will, but mine be done, O cosmic genie." This sets our Christian faith completely on its head.

Nevertheless, we do see something in this passage that may sound very much like that. It says, "He who sows sparingly will also reap sparingly, and he who sows bountifully will also reap bountifully." It sounds as if what we will receive is dependent upon what we give. In fact, this is precisely what Paul is saying! However, the difference here is what Paul states in the verse that follows: "And God is able to make all grace abound toward you, that you, always having all sufficiency in all things, may have an abundance for every good work" (2 Corinthians 9:8).

SELFISHNESS AND COVETOUSNESS

What is the purpose of our receiving from God? Is it selfishness? Is it for hoarding? Is it our own aggrandizement? Or is it from some higher purpose? The Bible says, "But seek first the kingdom of God and His righteousness, and all these things shall be added to you" (Matthew 6:33). It doesn't say, "Seek first a new Rolls Royce" or something like that; it's "Seek first the kingdom of God."

John Wesley once said, "But for **money** and the need ... **Make all you can**, save **all you can**, [and] give **all you can**." A lot of people get caught up with the first two and then change the third from "give all you can" to "spend all the money you can on yourself and your own pleasures!" Such people don't realize that they are caught up in something that is very pervasive, not only in the world, but also in the church—the problem of selfishness and covetousness. I have been in many prayer meetings, heard thousands of people pray, and heard people confess many sins, but I have never heard one person confess the sin of covetousness. How long has it been since you have confessed that sin? Yet, as one writer said, it is the most pervasive sin in all of the church.

The prevailing principle that existed before the fall of man, existing among the angels and the two people who were placed here in this world, was the *principle of love*. After the fall, the principle of love was changed into the *principle of selfishness*. In his excellent book, *Mammon or Covetousness, the Sin of the Christian Church*, Reverend John Harris says:

> Accordingly, *selfishness*, as we have already intimated, is the universal form of human depravity; every sin that can be named is only a modification of it. What is avarice, but selfishness grasping and hoarding? What is prodigality, but selfishness decorating and indulging itself—a man sacrificing to himself as his own god? What is sloth, but that god asleep, and refusing to attend to the loud calls of duty. And what is idolatry, but that god enshrined—man, worshipping the reflection of his own image? Sensuality, and, indeed, all the sins of the flesh, are only selfishness setting itself above law, and gratifying itself at the expense of all restraint. And all the sins of the spirit are only the same principle impatient of contradiction and refusing to acknowledge superiority or to bend to any will but its own. What is egotism, but selfishness speaking? Or crime, but selfishness without its mask in earnest and acting? Or offensive war, but selfishness confederated, armed and bent on aggrandizing itself by violence and blood?

BEWARE OF COVETOUSNESS

Indeed, all the sins of mankind can be traced to that root of selfishness. The Bible says that the *love of money* is the root of all sin. Actually, it says that the love of money is the root of *all kinds* of sin. Notice this—it doesn't say that money is the root of all sin. It is the *love* of money, or covetousness, which is the root of all sin. That is why Jesus said, "Beware of covetousness" (Luke 12:15).

In many different ways, selfishness, or covetousness, has enthroned itself in our lives. Like a vine, it has wrapped itself around various parts of our soul, choking life out of us. It manifests itself in many different forms every day of every week of our lives. Every time we are confronted with a decision, for example, to give money to the starving children of Ethiopia or to the hungry here at home, we have a struggle with selfishness in our own hearts. How do we do in that battle?

Every year we are confronted with making a decision in response to the questions: "What am I going to do for God and His Kingdom in this coming year? What kind of promise in faith am I going to make? What am I going to be willing to sacrifice in the coming year?" Each time we are confronted with these questions, the demon of selfishness rises up in our spirit and tries to strangle every effort of the *new principle of love* from expressing itself in the activities of our life.

As Rev. Harris said, every sin that can be named is only a modification of *selfishness*. If we were to analyze the very last sin of which we are conscious, we would again discover that selfishness, in one or another of its thousand forms, was its parent. Thus, if love was the pervading principle of the unfallen creation, it is equally certain that selfishness is the reigning law of the world—ravaged and disorganized by sin. Yet, most often we do not notice it in ourselves. So subtle is its influence, so pervasive its presence, and so frequent its manifestations that we are not even aware of its presence. Therefore, we can only be free from this by taking heed to what God has told us—He is able to give us *all* sufficiency in *all* things, if we will depend on Him. He is able to make His grace—the totally unmerited favor of God—abound toward us in every way.

THE BIBLICAL PRINCIPLE FOR FINANCIAL SUFFICIENCY

The grace of God is the attitude of God—the undeserved favor of God. However, God doesn't have idle dispositions. God always acts upon these and, therefore, His grace and His love are manifest in a thousand different forms. There is one "Grace," but there are a thousand graces that appear in so many different ways in our lives—like a meteor streaking through the heavens above without being seen until it hits the atmosphere, where it is suddenly ignited and seen in a thousand pinpoints of life. So the grace of God descends upon us in all sorts of different ways so that we, by that grace, should have *all* sufficiency in *all* things at *all* times.

But you may have noticed that Paul says that God *is able* to do this. He doesn't say that God necessarily *will* do it. There are conditions, the first of which is simply, "He who sows sparingly will also reap sparingly, and he who sows bountifully will also reap bountifully" (2 Corinthians 9:6). The average person of the world would be absolutely astonished at the biblical principle for financial success—for financial sufficiency—in this world. You could buy a hundred books on how to succeed in this world, read every one of them, and I assure you that it is very unlikely that you would find even one of them that would tell you that the great secret of succeeding is—by giving.

"He who sows bountifully will also reap bountifully." There have been those who have discovered that secret to be absolutely true. They have discovered that they cannot outgive God. In my experience, I have discovered over and over again—you cannot outgive God! And the more bountifully you sow, the more bountifully you will reap.

My friends, there are some of you who suffer from insufficiency. You have insufficiency in all things at all times. The reason is that you are robbing God. You are robbing God in your tithes and offerings. Even if you are getting by, you do not realize that covetousness has wrapped itself around your soul like a serpent and is strangling that new life that Christ would give you.

DIVINE RESTORATION OF BENEVOLENCE

If it is true that selfishness and covetousness are the basic malady we suffer in this world, the remedy for that sin must be calculated to get at the cause of the disease. It must restore to the world a lost sense of *benevolence*. In fact, the remedy provided gives us an unparalleled exhibition of God's divine grace. Indeed, the very depths of the ocean of God's being were stirred and the entire Trinity was moved into action to restore this benevolence. The very subsistence of Father, Son, and Holy Spirit began to act. The Father poured out the ocean of His love by doing that one thing which no earthly father could ever bring himself to do—give his only begotten son up to a cruel and hideous death.

The Son, Himself, came voluntarily to fulfill the Father's will. "I always do those things that please Him [my Father]" (John 8:29). He gave Himself for us: "In this is love, not that we loved God, but that He loved us and sent His Son to be the propitiation for our sins" (1 John 4:10). God in His infinite mercy came down into this world. He took our place in the universe. He absorbed all of our own interests. Our burden of guilt was imputed to Him, and He opened His bosom and took on that fatal stroke which our sins so condignly deserved. Jesus Christ manifested and exhibited a picture of undeserved love and benevolence the like of which the world had never seen before.

THE DESIRE TO GIVE

God not only gave us an exhibition of grace and love, He then sent the Holy Spirit, who came like a mighty wind to fill the hearts of those who have believed and to overpower them with a tremendous manifestation and realization. When we become personally acquainted with that love and know that it is for us that Christ died, He sets us aglow with that God-like spirit of giving. God fills the heart with such warmth of love that we desire to give—a desire that is foreign to the animal creation—for they are always gathering and hoarding. God, whose nature is to give, implants His same nature in us!

Diodorus Siculus wrote many centuries ago about a great forest fire in the Pyreneean Mountains of Spain. The intense blaze produced such tremendous heat that a huge deposit of silver below the surface of the ground, having reached the temperature for melting, gushed out of the mountain and revealed what was later found to be one of the largest silver deposits ever known. So it is when the heat of the Gospel comes into our life! When the fire of the cross touches our hearts, we, too, gush forth into acts of spontaneous giving and benevolence, as God slays that serpent of covetousness in us and enables us to be set free.

We become like God when we give like He has always given. We achieve self-sufficiency, *autarkeia*, as we learn to be like God and give bountifully. We are to sow bountifully that we might receive and harvest bountifully, in order that we may "abound to every good work." I have found that God pours out His blessings on Christians who are mature in the Lord—those who have learned to trust God. They do not covet the things of this world, but rather they delight in using that abundance for the advancement of the Kingdom of Jesus Christ and for the glory of His name. That is the type of person He would have you and me to become.

"Set your affection on things above, not on things on the earth," says the Bible (Colossians 3:2 KJV). Where have you set your affections? Is it your delight to trust God and receive abundance from Him, so that God may be glorified and lost people may be redeemed, and the Kingdom of Christ may be advanced? That is what it is all about in this world, my friends. If you are not becoming that kind of person, you are not becoming like God.

"And God is able to make all grace abound toward you;

that you, always having all sufficiency in all things, may have an abundance for every good work" (2 Corinthians 9:8). I hope you have grasped the secret of achieving all sufficiency: "He who sows sparingly will also reap sparingly, and he who sows bountifully will also reap bountifully" (2 Corinthians 9:6). Here is the great secret of getting and giving in this world. It is a great secret not only for supporting the work of Christ and for achieving self-sufficiency, but also for developing God-like personalities. May each one of us be able to rejoice in that all-sufficiency that comes from God, for He has dealt with every part of it. He has delivered us from covetousness and given a fatal stroke to the serpent of desire for money, and He can cause us to see that the great objective of life is the advancement of the Kingdom of God. As we reap bountifully, as we abound in this world, may we abound unto every good work, so that His name may be glorified!

Chapter Four

TAKING THE STRAIN OUT OF FINANCES

Life's one great lesson, Dr. Kennedy notes in this chapter, is to learn to "Trust God." Yet trusting Him for our finances seems to be the hardest lesson to learn—as demonstrated by the small percentage of born-again Christians who tithe.

If you've found it difficult to give the tithe, you'll find this chapter full of encouragement and exhortation. Dr. Kennedy shares his personal testimony of how he learned to tithe and shows the threefold blessing God has promised to those who do so—including "rebuking the devourer" for our sakes. Even when it seems like every time we turn around, the government has added another tax, and our retirement account is shrinking again, we can trust God to supply all our need.

"And my God shall supply all your need according to His riches in glory by Christ Jesus."
                                        —Philippians 4:19

Worry causes cavities. Perhaps you didn't know that, but a British clinic conducted lengthy studies and discovered that to be true. Anxiety, fear, and worry restrict the flow of saliva. As a result, acids in the mouth that corrode and eat teeth are not neutralized and cause tooth decay. Our stomachs are affected in much the same way. Worry also decreases eyesight. Dr. Leonard S. Fosdick of Northwestern University conducted studies which showed that one-third of all visual impairment is due to worry.

We have a God who loves us and that is exactly why He says over and over again, "Be anxious for nothing. Do not worry about anything. Fear not." God doesn't want us to worry. But rather He tells us, "Rejoice . . . and again I say, Rejoice" (Philippians 4:4). We can't worry and rejoice at the same time. We can't fear and rejoice at the same time. One supplants the other. If we don't understand this, we will never have the happy lives God wants us to have.

LIFE'S ONE GREAT LESSON

Life, essentially, is a school. The curriculum is broad, the subjects are many, and the courses are multitudinous, yet no matter what level of that school we're in, there is but one central lesson. That lesson is, "Trust me," says the Lord. God is calling upon us to trust Him. This is the secret of successful Christian living.

Many examinations occur in the school of life—tests that we must all pass or flunk. Whether they are tests in rearing babies or international relations, physical illnesses or mental depression, dating or dying, disciplining teenagers or running a corporation, the successful will always be those who learn *the lesson of trust*. I would like to apply that lesson by focusing a magnifying glass on one discipline, one course, one aspect of our lives—the very important matter of finances.

Many people spend much of their lives worrying about money. I know, because there was a time in my life many years ago when I did, too. It seemed I could never quite make ends meet. (By the way, experts tell us that worry about finances has less to do with how much we make and more to do with how we spend it, yet most Americans don't even have a budget. It's hard to be responsible with one's money without one.) Many people never learn the secret of trusting God for their finances, but instead, spend much of their lives worrying about them. You can either worry and be miserable, or you can trust and rejoice. If you worry and are miserable, you will likely become more miserable, because you will be faced with all sorts of other problems that worry causes, such as tooth caries and ulcers and impaired vision, to name a few.

A very famous author by the name of "Unknown," put it this way:

All the water in the world,
However hard it tried
Could never, never sink a ship
Unless it got inside.

And so it is with the problems of this world, they only sink us when they get inside of us!

PROMISES AND CONDITIONS

As with all of God's promises, there are conditions appended to them. For example, we are told, "Believe on the Lord Jesus Christ, and you will be saved" (Acts 16:31). This verse didn't say everyone was going to be saved. In fact, elsewhere it says, ". . . difficult is the way which leads to life, and there are few who find it" (Matthew 7:14). But I did say that all those who believe in Him shall be saved. We must fulfill the condition of faith in Christ. Then we may claim the promise and rejoice in it and be delivered from all worry about what is going to happen to us when we die and leave this world. I haven't the slightest worry about that, because I know He is going to take me to paradise to be with Him forever. That is the way it should be with all aspects of our lives, in every course in the school of life.

The condition in the area of our finances, however, is one that many people like to ignore. God has said, "'Bring all the tithes into the storehouse, . . . And try Me now in this,' says the Lord of hosts, 'If I will not open for you the windows of heaven and pour out for you *such* blessing that *there will* not *be room* enough *to receive it*'" (Malachi 3:10). We are to give, and on that basis we can claim His promise of abundant blessings. As Paul wrote to the Philippians, "My God shall supply all your need according to his riches in glory by Christ Jesus" (Philippians 4:19).

GOD IS THE GREATEST GIVER

Many people have a problem with greed and covetousness and, therefore, have great difficulty fulfilling the condition. But God is a God who gives! His greatest gift is His Son, and through Him, eternal life. "God so loved the world that He gave His only begotten son" (John 3:16). He is the Great Giver of every good and perfect gift.

God made the sun—it gives.
God made the moon—it gives.
God made the stars—they give.
God made the air—it gives.
God made the clouds—they give.
God made the earth—it gives.
God made the sea—it gives.
God made the trees—they give.
God made the flowers—they give.
God made the fowls—they give.
God made the beasts—they give.
God made the plants—they give.
God made man—and he gets everything he can and holds on to it—as hard and as long as he can!

I am reminded of one man whose entire life was spent "getting." He had a number of expensive "toys," as grown-up boys often do. After he died, his friends were astonished to see the size of the hole that had been dug for him at the cemetery. Then they saw the reason; the corpse was propped up behind the steering wheel of his gold Cadillac, and a crane was lowering the whole thing into the ground. Foolishly, this man had supposed that he could take his toys with him. But he, like everyone else of that mindset, was very, very wrong, and I have no doubt that he had much misery in his life as a result.

LEARNING TO GIVE

God wants us to become like Him, which means we have to learn to give. We have to learn to do what He has told us to do, "Bring all the tithes into the storehouse." A recent survey shows that many people in America today don't really know what God expects of them. Yet it is very clear that we are to bring the tithe and the offering.

What is a tithe? A *tithe is a tenth* of what we make—a tenth of our increase. Sometimes people say, "Oh, I believe in tithing; I just don't want anyone to tell me how much it should be!" My friends, a tithe doesn't mean simply "giving to God," nor does it mean "some portion" of your income. A tithe means specifically one thing and one thing only—it means a tenth. In the Hebrew it is *ma'aser* from *asar*, which means to give a tenth. In the Greek, it is *dekate*, which means a tenth. In the Old English it is *teotha*—a tenth. In Middle English it is *tethe*—a tenth, and finally, in modern English a "tithe" means a tenth.

God says that the earth and all its fullness belong to Him. He owns everything; He owns the cattle upon a thousand hills. There is nothing that really is ours. God created everything; therefore He owns everything, but He gives it to us as a stewardship. Yet He declares that the tithe belongs to Him. It is not negotiable. It is His and we are not to keep it. If we do, dire consequences follow.

A TRIPLE INDICTMENT

This is explained to us in Malachi 3:7-9. In this passage we see first of all a triple indictment. This is followed by a triple blessing in Malachi 3:10-12. In the threefold indictment, God says to His people, "Return to Me, and I will return to you." By this, He is declaring that they had departed from Him. They asked, however, "In what way shall we return?" Their consciences were so seared that, like many today, they didn't even know they had departed from God and were disobeying His basic financial commandment.

God replied, "Will a man rob God? Yet you have robbed Me."
And they said, "In what way have we robbed You?"
He said, "In tithes and offerings."

God's triple indictment against His people is: first, they had departed from God and his ordinances; second, they had robbed Him; and third, they were cursed with a curse, and that curse was very real and very painful. God says that they would gather together much and He would cause it to come to little. They would fill their hands, and He would blow on it and scatter it away. He says that they would put it in a bag, and He would put a hole in the bag. He said that He would send the locusts to eat up their crops, and what the locusts didn't eat, He would send the cankerworms to eat. He said, in effect, "Therefore, you will suffer want because you have departed from me, and you are robbing me." God is saying very clearly and without controversy in this passage in Malachi 3 that all those who withhold the tithe, which is His, are thieves—they are robbing Him.

One pastor of an upper middle class church that was having some financial difficulties did some computation. He figured that if all of the families of his church were reduced to the poverty level, and if they tithed on that amount, the church would have no financial problems at all. But many people are impeding the work of Christ, as well as bringing misery upon themselves, because they are not obeying God. Of course, the most important matter here is not the tithe itself, but the disobedience involved in withholding it.

Through disobedience, we are demonstrating an absence of faith in God's promise; we are showing ingratitude to God, who has given us everything to enjoy. We are showing a lack of love toward Him in whom we live and move and have our being. Still He doesn't crush us, but rather He calls us to repentance. "'Return to Me and I will return to you,' says the Lord of hosts." If we but repent of this sin and return to Him, He will open the windows of heaven and pour out a blessing upon us!

A THREEFOLD BLESSING

Now note the threefold blessing. First, He says that hereby they may "try" God and thus strengthen their faith. They may become greater witnesses to all those they know as it becomes evident that God has blessed their faith and fidelity to Him. This is the only place in the Bible where God says "try me." In the King James Version it says "prove me." Would you like to prove God? "Bring ye all the tithes into the storehouse . . . and prove me now herewith, saith the Lord of hosts, if I will not open you the windows of heaven, and pour you out a blessing, that there shall not be room enough to receive it" (Malachi 3:10 KJV).

Second, God says that this blessing will come from open windows in Heaven. How many people pray to God, and it seems that the heavens are brass and there is no answer because they are living in disobedience. They have departed from God, and they don't know it. They are not keeping His ordinance and, therefore, He does not hear their prayers. To those who are obedient to God, however, the windows will be opened, and the blessing will be such that "there shall not be room enough to receive it."

Third, God says, "I will rebuke the devourer for your sakes" (Malachi 3:11). He is talking about the devourer of the ground who devours the fruit of their field—who causes the vines to cast their fruit before the season. We do not live in an agricultural community, but there are still things that devour our lives and our livelihood. Many people have disobeyed God and have withheld the tithe, thinking that would bring an advantage. Nevertheless, they have spent five or ten times over their tithe on doctors' bills, because the devourer of their lives has not been rebuked by God. Rather, due to their disobedience, it has been unleashed. Their own personal cankerworms and locusts are consuming them. Many people rob God of His tithe and then wonder why nothing goes right in their business. They don't know that they have departed from God and are under His financial curse when, instead, they could be under His blessing. Why would anyone want to miss out on that blessing?

NOT A MATTER OF FINANCE

My friends, note very well—tithing is not a matter of finance. There are some who say they don't make enough money to tithe. Yet if God says He is going to curse us if we don't tithe, and if He promises that if we do tithe, He will bless us with blessings such that there will not be room enough to receive it, who can afford not to tithe?

Some people say they don't make *enough* money to tithe; some people say they make *too much* money to tithe! I think of one man who told Peter Marshall, former Chaplain of the Senate, that he started tithing in his church and God started blessing him and blessing him over the years. First thing you know, he was making $500,000 a year! He came to Reverend Marshall and said, "Dr. Marshall, you know that I've been tithing for years, but I just make so much right now, I can't afford to give that much money away."

Dr. Marshall said, "Well, I certainly can understand how you would feel about that. Why don't we go to God in prayer?"

He said, "Dear Lord, reduce this man's income down to the

place that he can afford to tithe again."

Maybe He is doing that to some of you right now. Tithing is not a matter of finance; it is a matter of faith—of simply taking God at His word. Do you believe He keeps His word?

THE SURPRISES TITHING BRINGS

Someone has said that a number of surprises come with tithing. Those that begin to tithe are usually surprised—although they really shouldn't be—at the amount of money they have left for the Lord's work. They are surprised at the way their spiritual life and faith are deepened as they tithe. They are surprised at the ease they have at meeting their own obligations with the remaining nine-tenths, which always seems to go farther than the whole ten. They are also surprised at the ease they experience in going from one-tenth to a larger percentage of their income. They are surprised at the preparation this gives to be a faithful and wise steward over their remaining money. Finally, they are surprised at themselves for waiting so long to adopt tithing!

A survey conducted in twenty-one universities showed in an examination of five hundred college students, that those who worried about money and worried about all sorts of other things made the lowest grades in the class. When will we learn the lesson that a loving Father so wants to teach us, which is "how to take the strain out of finances"? My friend, obey God's command—His ordinance. Bring the tithes and the offerings into His storehouse and trust Him in His work. He will provide for all of your needs out of his riches in glory. He will open the windows of heaven and pour out such a blessing that there will not be room enough to receive it!

PERSONAL TESTIMONY

May I share just a word, finally, of personal testimony?

When I became a Christian, I remember giving ten dollars a week to the Lord's work, and I remember how painful that was! It just seemed like it was wrenched from my hand every Sunday when I gave it away. Then I heard about tithing. What a positively agonizing thought! I could understand that Scotsman who, when he heard about "giving 'til it hurts," said, "Aye, mon, the very idea hurts!" Well, it hurt me too, because I always had trouble making ends meet. Then I learned to give, and what's more, I learned that I can't out-give God! I learned that He gives back far more than I can give to Him, so I was able to increase the tithe more and more and more, until that ten dollars a week increased many, many times over that amount. Now God continues to open the windows of heaven and provide for me from sources I never even dreamt existed. He will do the same for anyone who will trust Him and take Him at His word.

So I would ask you which most typifies your life: Worry? Anxiety? Fear? Or Joy? Rejoicing? Gladness? The latter is what God wants for you. Why don't you take Him at His word? Learn life's one great lesson—trust Him, and He will bless you! Even when we are anxious and worried during these difficult days, God our Father is able to provide for us just as in any other days. There is no exhausting of His resources—He owns the cattle upon a thousand hills! Let us, therefore, remember to thank Him as He so wondrously provides for all of those who are faithful to do what He has told us to do.

Chapter Five

OPEN THE WINDOWS OF HEAVEN

*The tithe is just one part of Christian stewardship, yet it is so pivotal that we neglect it to our own peril. As the previous chapter showed, if we expect God to supply our needs, as He promises in Philippians 4:19, we cannot rob Him of the tithe. The point should not be missed, either, that such New Testament promises do not abrogate the tithe; rather, they presuppose it. Therefore, it is fitting that this book includes two chapters in which Dr. Kennedy expounds on these bedrock verses in Malachi 3. In this chapter, Dr. Kennedy shows that God identified a **Problem** among His people. Then He gave them a **Prescription** to solve it, which was the condition for receiving a marvelous **Promise** of blessings. Do we, His people—the church of Jesus Christ, not see this same problem among us today? Let us follow His divine prescription, so that we may have the windows of heaven opened to us, and the blessings poured out upon us!*

"'Bring all the tithes into the storehouse, that there may be food in my house, and try me now in this,' says the Lord of hosts, 'If I will not open for you the windows of heaven and pour out for you such a blessing, that there shall not be room enough to receive it.'"
—*Malachi 3:10*

In Malachi 3:8, God asks a very penetrating question, "Will a man rob God?" Now, you might think this would be the height of folly, and yet robbers are sometimes noted for their folly. Paul Harvey told of the man who went into a bank with his face covered so that he couldn't be recognized or identified if a picture were taken of him. He had the people lie on the floor. He got away with the money. No one saw his face, no one saw his car, no one saw which way he went, but in robbing the bank, he had given the teller one of his personal checks with the words, "Give me all your money!" written on the back. How foolish can one be!

Another young bank robber told the teller to give him her car keys, along with the money. He ran out of the bank and got into her car. Ten minutes later the police converged on the car with its motor roaring, and the young man frantically trying to get the car moving. When the policeman stepped up to the window with his gun drawn, the young man, with great frustration in his voice, asked him, "What is this thing?" The policeman responded, "That, young man, is called a gear shift. Please step out of the car."

Foolish, you say, and, indeed, they were. Yet how much more foolish are we if we are robbing God! We cannot possibly hide our identity, nor is there anywhere that we can flee so that He cannot find us, nor is there any possibility of our escaping His judgment and condemnation. Yet God says, "Will a man rob God? Yet you have robbed Me! But you say, 'In what way have we robbed You?' In tithes and offerings. You are cursed with a curse, for you have robbed Me, even this whole nation" (Malachi 3:8-9).

There are three central points made in this section of Malachi 3 that I would like to share with you. First of all, there is the *problem*, then the *prescription*, and then the *promise*.

THE PROBLEM

The *problem* is that they had robbed God, and the curse of

God hung over their heads and caused them and their nation to languish. It was a curse upon their financial well-being. Their vines had been casting forth their fruit before the season. Various kinds of pests had been eating up their crops. The whole nation was languishing in a great financial decline because they had been robbing God, and the curse of God rested upon them.

Now, most of us don't live in an agricultural community, but let me tell you this—there are more parts of God's curse than either you or I could even begin to count. God has modern forms of locusts and cankerworms. There is that unexpected bill from the IRS. There is that sudden hospitalization, and when discharged, a bill for $10,000, and you were only there for two nights. There are a thousand and one other things God can do. To paraphrase Haggai 1:6-9, God says, "You think it will come to much, and I'll cause it to come to little. You put it [wages] into a bag, and I'll put a hole in the bag. You gather it together, and I'll blow on it and it will disappear." It's a terrible thing to live our lives under the financial curse of God, but some of you are doing just that.

A tithe, of course, means a *tenth*. That's what it means in English, Anglo-Saxon, Greek, Hebrew, Latin, and all languages. It means a tenth of our income. Someone asked if that means the net or the gross. Well, do you want God's blessing on your net or on your gross? Of course, it means the gross. A *tithe* is a tenth and an *offering* is that which we give beyond the tithe. Anything less than that is a heist; it is robbing God. Yet many people wonder why they just can't seem to make ends meet. They get all dressed up and come to church on Sunday morning, and then they put their hand in God's cash register and rob Him! Some of you did it today. "You are cursed with a curse, for you have robbed Me, even this whole nation," says God (Malachi 3:9).

God wants us to understand that He is the sovereign ruler and owner of this world. As a well-known hymn says: "This is my Father's world: I rest me in the thought." God is simply letting us use His world for a while. We're like a steward who is given a large estate to manage and is then to give a proper portion of the income to the owner.

Jesus told the story of a wealthy man who planted a great vineyard. He walled it around and built a tower on it. Then he leased it out to some men with the understanding they would return to him the proper percentage of the income. However, they didn't do it, so he sent a messenger, and they killed the messenger. He sent another messenger, and they killed him too. Finally, he sent his son, and they killed his son! The owner said, "What shall I do with these?" He said, "I will destroy these wicked men and give the vineyard to others who are more worthy." How do you figure in that parable, my friend? By the tithe we acknowledge God's sovereign ownership of this earth and all that is within it.

God wants us to learn to trust Him. There is one great lesson to be learned in this world and that is to trust God. That is the subject of the whole curriculum, and tithing is one of the courses on how to do it—and a very important one it is! My friend, if you can't trust God for the next three months, how can you say that you trust Him for the next three trillion years? How can you say you believe that when you step out of this world in death that He is going to be there to take care of you, when you can't even step out for the next week without robbing Him?

Tithing is a great lesson in faith. Remember that tithing is not a matter of finances; it is simply a matter of faith, because God says that we are not the loser. If we tithe, He will open the windows of heaven and pour out a blessing upon us. If we don't, we live under His curse. So the person who says "I can't afford to tithe," should ask himself, "Can I afford to live under the curse of God? Can I afford not to tithe, if God promises to bless me when I do?" If we do not believe His Word is true in this, then why should we claim to believe that any of God's promises are true?

God wants to use this method for the advancement of His kingdom here on earth. This is the way He does it. God doesn't need anything, but God has chosen to allow us to have a part in winning men and women to Christ all over the world. Therefore, when you withhold your tithe, you not only bring the curse upon yourself and your family, but also upon others all over the world who will not hear the gospel. Just think how vastly greater could be the churches' influence if all Christians tithed!

I saw a bumper sticker some years ago that said, "Honk if you love Jesus." Then another bumper sticker came along in the battle of the bumper stickers that said, "Tithe if you love Jesus. Anybody can honk." Well, these days there are a lot of people who come to church on Sunday and honk the hymns and make a great noise, but they don't tithe.

We can tithe without loving Christ, but we can't love Christ without tithing. Jesus said, "If you love Me, keep My commandments" (John 14:15). He said to the Pharisees, "Woe to you, scribes and Pharisees, hypocrites! For you pay tithe of mint and anise and cumin, . . ." The scribes and Pharisees were scrupulous about their tithing, right down to the garden herbs; but notice what they missed, ". . . and have neglected the weightier *matters* of the law: justice and mercy and faith. These you ought to have done, without leaving the others undone" (Matthew 23:23). Notice, Jesus said, "These you ought to have done, without leaving the others undone." By the way, the word "ought" used here has the same root as the word "must" found in John 3:7, when He says, "You *must* be born again."

My friend, do you really love Christ? That should be the motive for our giving. Our motive for giving should not be to get, but to show our love. God so loved that He gave. We should so love that we give. Yet, amazingly, when we do give, God has arranged it so that we don't lose anything, because He promises to bless us!

THE PRESCRIPTION

The problem described in Malachi 3 is that His people had robbed God, and the curse of God hung over their heads and caused them and their nation to languish. But this chapter also contains a *prescription*—or a solution to the problem. God said, "Bring all the tithes into the storehouse" (Malachi 3:10). The storehouse was a storehouse in the temple—the treasury where Jesus watched the people throwing their gifts into the great treasury, when He commended the widow who gave her last mite.

People sometimes ask me, "Do you think I should give my tithe to the church or to other organizations?" God said to bring the tithe into the storehouse. I have always seen that I give at least the tithe and even many times over that to the church, and then give other offerings to other organizations. But certainly the tithe should go to the church.

Remember, the tithe is not just a part of the Mosaic Law. Abraham gave tithes to Melchizedek, who was a type of Christ. We read in Genesis that Jacob continued the tithe. Moses commanded it. The tithe is holy unto the Lord, and should be given, as Malachi declares quite emphatically: "Bring all the tithes into the storehouse." Jesus commended it in the New Testament, and in the early church numerous church fathers point out that the tithe continues. It is timeless. From the beginning to this day, the tithe has been a part of the worship of the people of God.

"Bring all the tithes into the storehouse *that there may be food in my house.*" This phrase simply means that the work of the temple or the church may continue. This is so sadly neglected that many churches languish because of the covetousness of the people who do not give their tithes to God. As a result, the work of Christ does not go on. Jesus said, "Beware of covetousness [or greed]" (Luke 12:15). If you are not tithing, you are not only withholding the blessing of God from yourself, but you are also withholding the blessing of God from others, because ministry is limited by a lack of funds. That is true in churches all over the country today.

THE PROMISE

"And try Me now in this," the verse continues. It is incredible that God allows Himself to be put in the dock and to be tried and proved. What an amazing thing that is! This is the only place in the Bible where God says, "Try me" or "Prove me" (as it says in the King James Version.) Many times you hear unbelievers say, "*Prove* that there is a God." Well, God tells you a way of doing it. "Try Me [prove Me] now in this. . . if I will not open for you the windows of heaven, and pour out for you such a blessing, that there will not be room enough to receive it" (Malachi 3:10).

The words "windows of heaven," interestingly, are the same words that are used in Genesis 7 in speaking about the flood in Noah's day. God opened the "windows of heaven" and the water poured out, and for forty days the world was covered with water. The windows opened and God's *wrath* fell upon the earth because "the wickedness of man *was* great in the earth, and every intent of the thoughts of his heart *was* only evil continually" (Genesis 6:5).

However, now God promises to open the windows of heaven and pour out a *blessing* upon us. What an amazing condescension! God had said that the tithe was holy unto Him, that it belonged to Him, that it was not to be withheld. They were to give it, and when they did not, He extended His curse upon them. All He needed to do was simply stop right there. "Continue to disobey me and you will be cursed."

But God goes beyond that. He says that He will bless those who obey His command and bless them so abundantly that there will not be room enough to receive it! Indeed, many people have experienced the reality of that blessing, and I know that in my own life this has been true. God has blessed me more and more. The more I have given, the more He has blessed me.

John Bunyan, the author of *Pilgrim's Progress*, penned a little couplet that each of you ought to inscribe in your mind and not forget.

There was a man; some called him "mad."
The more he gave, the more he had!

Tithing is simply remaining legitimate and not being a criminal in the sight of God. Tithing keeps us from becoming guilty of robbing God. However, it is the *offering* which is given above the tithe that shows the true extent of our love and faith in God. I have discovered that as I have gone beyond the tithe, God's blessings have been exceedingly multiplied in my life. I can happily say that I may be counted among those "mad" men of whom Bunyan spoke: "There was a man; some called him 'mad.' The more he gave, the more he had." Are you among the group that the world calls mad?

SHOWING OUR GRATITUDE

Robert Laidlaw, an Australian writer, tells about visiting a family who had a five- or six-year-old girl. He brought a little box of chocolates with him. He gave them to the girl and her eyes lit up and she took them and ran into the next room. Laidlaw continued talking with her parents. About twenty minutes later, she came back with chocolate all over her lips and her fingers.

The following week, he visited another home, which also had a girl about the same age. He brought another box of chocolates and gave them to her. Her eyes lit up and she opened the box eagerly. Then she said to him, "Here, you have the first one."

Laidlaw said, "No, no, no, I brought them for you."

"No, I want *you* to have the first one," she insisted. He took the first candy.

He later said, "Guess which little girl won my heart?" And guess which little girl got another box of candy? My friends, is the chocolate showing on your lips?

Jesus told the parable about ten lepers who were healed, and only one came back to thank Him for healing them. Jesus asked "But where are the nine?" (Luke 17:17). Where are those who show their gratitude by obeying Him and bringing their tithes and offerings unto the Lord?

GOLD FOR IRON

In 1813, the country of Prussia was engaged in war. The king, Frederick William III, was trying to end the war and he was also trying to build up the nation to make it a great nation, but there was little money in the treasury. Therefore, the king decided to appeal to the women of the country. He asked them to bring in their gold jewelry. When they did so, they each received a piece of iron jewelry in its place. On its back was inscribed, "I gave gold for iron. 1813." These iron pieces were in the shape of a cross, and this was the beginning of the famous "Order of the Iron Cross." The women wore these iron crosses around their necks with more pride than they had when wearing their former gold jewelry. Perhaps we need a similar "Order of the Cross of Christ" consisting of those who give their tithes and offerings. There would be a major difference in this order, however. In our case, we give *iron* to the Lord and He gives *gold* back to us! He has given us His promise, "I will . . . open you the windows of heaven and pour out a blessing."

Have you experienced that promise, my friend? If you have been faithful, you have indeed, and you know that He is able to meet your needs. That doesn't mean that there aren't times when God may hide His face from us and cause us to walk in darkness to test us. Remember, the lesson is "trust God." It is said that God hid His face from Hezekiah that He might know everything that was in his heart. God was testing Hezekiah's motives to see if he really loved Him.

The purpose of giving to the Lord is to glorify God. It is to show our gratitude and our thankfulness. It is to advance the work of the cause of Christ. It is not simply to "get." Yet, even then God continues to give. Nevertheless, God does test us from time to time to see if our motives are really right in this matter. Then He comes back, and He continues to open the windows of heaven.

THE PROMISE REPEATED

This promise is repeated in many places—not just in Malachi:

- Honor the Lord with your possessions, and with the firstfruits of all your increase; so your barns will be filled with plenty, and your vats will overflow with new wine (Proverbs 3:9-10).

- One gives freely, yet grows all the richer; another withholds what he should give, and only suffers want (Proverbs 11:24 ESV).

- Give, and it will be given to you: good measure, pressed down, shaken together, and running over will be put into your bosom. For with the same measure that you use, it will be measured back to you (Luke 6:38).

These promises are opposite of the world's wisdom. The world says: "Hold on to it and you shall have." God says, "Give it away and you shall have." Remember:

There was a man; some called him "mad."
The more he gave, the more he had.

Are you missing out on the blessings of God? Are you causing others to miss out on the Gospel of salvation? You have an opportunity this week to do more than simply "honk if you love Jesus." You have the opportunity to prove it and to prove Him by bringing your tithes into the storehouse. May God grant you the grace of giving, so that you may experience the joy of knowing that God is real, that He will never leave you nor forsake you, and that you cannot outgive Him! For we have His promise that He will, indeed, open the windows of heaven and pour out such a blessing that there will not be room enough to receive it.

Chapter Six

THE CONSECRATED THING

Although the tithe is of primary importance, it is only a part of the larger picture of Christian stewardship. In this chapter Dr. Kennedy sets forth five principles of stewardship, noting that in a nation that has become for the most part "spiritually illiterate," few understand these principles today, much less apply them.

This sermon was preached in 1995. That was the year the Internet stock market boom took off. How might our nation look today if those who profited from that boom had understood these principles of stewardship and applied them?

"Therefore the children of Israel could not stand before their enemies, but turned their backs before their enemies, because they have become doomed to destruction. Neither will I be with you anymore, unless you destroy the accursed from among you."
                                                                        —Joshua 7:12

Today is "Stewardship Sunday." Once a year on this day, we talk about our responsibilities to God as His stewards. I have frequently discussed the matter of tithing on this day. However, given that we now live in a nation that is for the most part spiritually illiterate—a nation where every effort has been made to remove the Bible not only from the schools, but from the minds of people—there are now many who do not understand the larger principles of stewardship, of which tithing is but one part. Therefore, in order to see the larger context of tithing, we will look at these general principles of stewardship that are given to us in the Bible. For God expects us to follow these in our lives.

FIVE PRINCIPLES

"The earth is the LORD's, and all its fullness." This verse, found in 1 Corinthians 10:26, reminds us that all that is in the world is God's. God is the Creator. He has created all things: the galaxies, the stars, the firmament, and all that exists. He created this earth upon which He placed us. He made it, He owns it, He possesses it, it belongs to Him—as do we. Therefore, we need to acknowledge in our lives that there is nothing that is ultimately our own. We have received all that we have as a *stewardship* from God.

A *steward* is one who deals with, occupies, and handles property that belongs to another. The steward must give an account to the owner of how he has dealt with it. "The earth is the Lord's and all its fullness." We need to remember that there is nothing we can give to God that is our own. God has given us all we have. The Scripture says, *"It is He who gives you power to get wealth"* (Deuteronomy 8:18). Therefore, we do not give ours to Him; we simply return His to the One who gave it to us in the first place. That is the first principle of biblical stewardship.

God wants us, not ours. 2 Corinthians 8:5 states, "They first gave themselves to the Lord, and *then* to us by the will of God." This verse, which speaks of stewardship and giving various things to the needs of the poor, affirms that God is far more interested in *us* than in any "things" we may have in our possessions.

God has created us in His own image. Therefore, we must first give ourselves to Him. Until we have first given ourselves unto Him—until we have been cleansed by the blood of Christ and sanctified by the Holy Spirit, anything we give unto God is an abomination. It comes from an unclean heart and a mind whose motives are principally selfish. Therefore, it is not acceptable to God. It is only after He has accepted *us* that He can or will accept *ours*.

The principle of the "firstfruits" is taught throughout the Bible. God has said that our first fruits belong to Him. This means that we demonstrate our acknowledgement that the earth is the Lord's and the fullness thereof by returning unto Him what He requires, namely the first fruits of all that He gives to us. We are not to give the middle fruits, or the last fruits, or the fruits that are there "after I see if I am going to have something left over." No, we start in faith by giving to Him our *first* fruits.

The Bible describes the *firstfruits* as the tithe and the offering. A tithe, according to the meaning of the word in Hebrew, Greek, Latin, and English is a tenth of all that God gives to us—a tenth of all of our income. An offering is anything we give over that tenth. Anything less than that, Malachi reminds us, is nothing but a theft. "Will a man rob God? Yet you have robbed Me! But you say, 'In what way have we robbed You?' In tithes and offerings. You are cursed with a curse, for you have robbed Me" (Malachi 3:8-9).

The tithe is a test. During the Cold War, on television and radio, from time to time a voice would come on and say, "This is a test." It was a test of the emergency broadcast system. Well, my friends, the tithe is a test. A test of what? It is a test of the reality of your faith. This is why Christ talked far more about possessions and money than even about heaven and hell. Our handling of our possessions is a visible, tangible representation of the reality of our faith. Whatever you trust in is your god. Who is your god? What is your god? Is it the true God, or is it gold—money—mammon? We are told, "You cannot serve God and mammon" (Mark 6:24). Whatever we trust in for our well-being is our god.

This is why the Bible says several times that neither adulterers, nor fornicators, nor thieves, nor murderers, nor the covetous man who is an idolater—none of these have any inheritance in the kingdom of God. The covetous man *is* an idolater. The covetous man hoards all of the gifts God has given to him. Because of his covetousness he does not return unto God the tithe or the offering, and thereby he shows that he has placed his trust in gold rather than in God. By definition, he is an idolater. Note well, dear friend, no idolater will ever enter into Heaven, and therefore, the covetous man who is an idolater has no inheritance in the kingdom of God.

Every Sunday the test of the tithe is given. It was given this morning when the offering plate was passed. People will stand and sing and profess their faith and recite their belief, but do they tithe? It doesn't matter what we say with our lips; the reality or unreality of our faith and trust in God is made plain every time that plate passes by. We're not graded A, B, or C; it's a "pass-fail" test.

Wonderful blessings await us. What do we receive if we pass the test of the tithe? We have God's promise that wonderful blessings will be ours. "'Bring all the tithes into the storehouse, that there may be food in My house, and try Me now in this,' says the LORD of hosts, 'If I will not open for you the windows of heaven and pour out for you *such* blessing that *there will* not *be room* enough *to receive it*'" (Malachi 3:10).

Can you image not having enough storerooms to receive all of God's blessings? Can you imagine "the windows of heaven" opening up to pour out God's blessings? That's what God promises to those who tithe.

In summary, then, the five principles of stewardship we've seen here include:

- The earth is the Lord's.

- God wants *us* before *ours*.

- We are to bring the first fruits of all that we receive.

- These fruits are defined in the test of the tithe.

- If we pass the test, there are great blessings in store for us.

A PICTURE WRIT LARGE

Some of you are no doubt wondering how all of the above relates to our text, and the battle at Ai recorded in the seventh chapter of Joshua. We have all heard about the battle of Jericho described in the preceding chapter. Since we were little children, we heard that "Joshua fit the battle of Jericho, . . . and the walls came a 'tumblin' down." What does it mean? Most people do not realize that the whole inheritance of the Promised Land is a great picture "writ large" of the five principles of stewardship we just outlined above.

"The earth is the Lord's and all its fullness." This was true of Canaan as well. Canaan did and does belong to the Lord. He had "rented it out" to some inhabitants, including the Philistines, Hivites, Hittites, and lots of other "ites." However, these people had shown themselves to be unfit "renters," and they were, indeed, abominations in the sight of God—so much so that previously God had said that the land was not yet ready for the Israelites to enter, because the cup of the wrath of the Amorites was not yet full. But now it was. We are told elsewhere that the inhabitants were virtually vomited out of the land because of their sin.

Jericho was but a short walk from the site where the Canaanite god Molech was worshipped outside of Jerusalem. You might recall that these people worshiped a huge hollow bronze statue of the god Molech, with his hands extended. A tremendous fire would be built inside the belly of the statue until the whole idol glowed red hot. Then on those waiting red-hot hands, the people would place their babies. The beating of drums would drown out the screams of the dying infants. Indeed, the land vomited out its inhabitants! God was sending them an eviction notice—and the sheriff was Joshua and the people of Israel.

God wants us before ours. When the Israelites crossed the Jordan, they came to Gilgal. There the men were circumcised, because they had not been practicing circumcision during their forty years of wandering in the desert. So, the very first thing they did was to commit themselves unto the Lord. Circumcision, which is the Old Testament symbol for what we now practice as baptism, symbolized the committal of the individual unto God. We read in the New Testament, "they first gave themselves to the Lord," (2 Corinthians 8:5). Thus did the Israelites commit themselves to Him.

Give the first fruits. This was the beginning of God giving unto the people, and He demanded that the first fruits be returned unto Him. That first city was Jericho, which now lay under the hand of God. These pagans were cursed by God for their sins, and they were to be utterly destroyed.

To that end God demonstrated a miracle, and the walls came tumbling down when Joshua and the people compassed the city. The priests sounded on the ram's horn and the sheep horn and the walls crashed downward. The people clamored over the walls and destroyed the inhabitants. But they had been warned that everything there was accursed. They were not to touch it. The gold and the silver were to be placed into the treasury of the Lord. It was the "consecrated thing."

Then we read the tragic case of Achan. Achan came up with the rest of the soldiers into Jericho. When the city was taken, he saw among the spoils a beautiful Babylonian garment. It must have been, indeed, a beautiful thing to behold—Hart, Shaffner & Marx, no doubt—with threads of silver and gold. He coveted this colorful garment. Then he saw shekels of silver and a wedge of gold. He gathered it all up carefully, wrapped it in the garment, put it under his robe, and hurried back to his tent. He made his way inside and looked around. "Nobody saw me," he thought. He dug a hole in the ground, and into it he put the gold and silver and the garment, and then covered it all over, smoothed it out, put a piece of carpet over it, and sat down and caught his breath. He was sure no one had seen him. However, just as in the case of David, when he thought he had gotten away with his sin, "the thing that David had done displeased the Lord" (2 Samuel 11:27), and the eyes of God had seen it all.

We may "get away with" our sins here in this world, but the eyes of God see all. The thing that Achan did displeased the Lord. Therefore, when the army went up to the little town of Ai, which they expected to easily take, the men of this small town came out and routed the army of Israel and caused them to turn and flee. The children of Israel were now accursed by God, and He was no longer with them. Thirty-six men died in the field that day because of the sin of Achan. I sometimes wonder how many times the church does not advance as it ought to advance; it does not grow as it ought to grow; it does not conquer as it ought to conquer, because there is an Achan in its midst. Alas, perhaps a number of them have hidden "the consecrated thing" in their tents.

Is your spiritual name Achan? I had a friend, now deceased, whose parents, to my utter astonishment, had named him Achan. Why would any parent name their son after one who had so disgraced the armies of Israel and brought such destruction upon himself? Yet some of you have done the same thing. When Achan finally was pointed out by the finger of God and exposed for his sin, Joshua called upon him to confess and give glory to God. So he did, and he said, "I *saw* the garment and the gold, and I *coveted* it, and I *took* it, and I *hid* it" (Joshua 7:21 paraphrased).

From the very beginning, that is the way it always goes. Eve *saw* the fruit of the tree, and she *coveted* it, seeing that it was good to eat, and it was delightful to the eye, and it was good to make one wise. Having coveted it, she *took* it, ate it, and then, with her husband, she *hid* among the trees of the garden.

The test of the tithe. Oh, Achan, do you not know that you cannot hide from God? You have looked upon the gold and silver that God has given you the power to get. You have coveted it for yourself—even that part which is devoted unto God, the tithe. You have taken it, and you have hidden it in your bank account, in your portfolio, under your mattress, or wherever. You've said, "Nobody saw me." But the thing you have done displeases the Lord. Each Sunday you come, and you flunk the test, and what is the consequence? In Haggai 1:6, God says:

> *You have sown much, and bring in little;*
> *You eat, but do not have enough;*
> *You drink, but you are not filled with drink;*
> *You clothe yourselves, but no one is warm;*
> *And he who earns wages,*
> *Earns wages to put into a bag with holes.*

You may think that your efforts will bring in much, but when you rob God, your efforts will bring in little. You may try to save it and put it into a bag, and He will put a hole in the bag. You may suppose that you can become wealthy enough so you won't have to trust in the Lord to provide for your needs, and you won't need to be submissive to Him because, after all, you have provided for your own needs. But, my friends, God can put a hole in your bag. You may say, "Not in my bag. It's stainless steel." Well, God *can* put a hole in your bag! God can bring a disease on you that all the money in the world cannot heal. God has 40 trillion ways of exercising His displeasure with you. You want to prove how many He has? He can make you so miserable that you won't care how much you have in that stainless steel box; it won't mean a thing to you. You have *seen*, you have *coveted*, you have *taken*, and you have *hidden*. But the thing you have done displeases the Lord.

So what happened to Achan? When the finger of God pointed him out, he was brought forth. He and his family with him were taken and stoned to death. Their bodies were burned and covered over with stones. Not only did Achan bring destruction upon himself and his family, but he brought destruction upon the armies of God. There are many people who are hurting the work of Christ because of the Achan spirit in their hearts. The greatest tragedy, however, is how much they themselves have missed because they have not trusted in God. God said to Joshua and the people that He would no longer be with them until they had gotten rid of the accursed thing. When they did so, God was with them again, and they went on from victory unto victory, from conquest unto conquest.

Great blessings for faith. Those who will trust in the Lord will find that He will, indeed, "open for you the windows of heaven and pour out for you *such* blessing that *there will* not *be room* enough *to receive it.*" Trusting in Him is a test of faith, and it proves whether our god is gold or the true God—whether we worship God or mammon.

Dear friend, how are you doing in the test of stewardship? Did you flunk the test today? Last week? Last month? Last year? May God grant you the faith to trust Him for all things, to experience that it is from the great God that all blessings flow, and He will pour out His blessings upon your life. He wants to bless you, but those blessings come only through true faith, and the evidence of that faith is seen in the tithe. When we pass that test, we can look forward confidently and joyfully, in faith, to the outpourings of His blessings from Heaven.

Chapter Seven

STANDING ON THE PROMISES

The Bible contains over eight thousand promises, and, as Dr. Kennedy points out in the beginning of this chapter, very few of these are promises made to God by men. By nature we are all promise-breakers. Therefore, if, after reading the preceding chapters, you promised God that you would begin to tithe, don't look to your own ability to keep that promise. Stand on His promises, not your own. Look up to God and see all that He has promised us as a part of our inheritance in Christ.

"For all the promises of God in Him are Yes, and in Him Amen, to the glory of God through us."
—II Corinthians 1:20

I f you consider the ancient pagan religions, such as the religions of the Greeks and Romans, you will find that there were many gods and many promises involved. You will also discover that almost all of them were promises made by men to the gods, and very, very few were promises made by the gods unto men. Contrariwise, there are in the Scriptures over 8,000 promises, almost all of which are promises made by God unto men, and very few that have been made by men unto God.

In fact, the New Testament contains scores of promises made by God unto men. However, there is not, to my knowledge, one single promise made by a Christian person to God in the entire New Testament. Many people in today's churches think that the essence of Christianity involves making promises to God. They promise to do better, and they are really sorry. They promise that they are going to turn over a new leaf, they are going to follow more dutifully, and they are going to do all of these things. Yet you don't find this among the Christians in the New Testament. Instead, all you find are promises made by God to men.

There are also a few promises made by ungodly people to other people, such as the promise of the chief priests and Pharisees to give money to Judas to betray Christ. There were certain Jews who promised they were going to kill Paul. Certain false teachers who "crept into the houses" of foolish women, promised them liberty, but led them deeper into the bondage of sin. There are such promises as that. But we do not find promises made by the Christians unto God—not a one.

So consider this—if you think that Christianity is tied up with making a lot of promises to God, sort of like an extended New Year's Eve, I would say that your religion is closer to the ancient pagan religions of the Greeks and Romans. It is not the New Testament religion of Christ.

BY FAITH ALONE—OF GRACE ALONE

Why is that? Because, as Paul said, we stand by faith. Many people don't know that we are not saved by our striving, our efforts, our turning over new leaves, but we are saved by faith in Jesus Christ. We are justified by faith. Justification by faith alone was the great watchword of the Protestant Reformation. However, even most Protestants today have lost their hold on that great truth. Nevertheless, it still holds.

The question we must then ask is, "Why has God arranged that we are justified by faith?" It would seem that He should do the thing that seems most obvious to most people. The Scripture says, "There is a way *that seems* right to a man" (Proverbs 14:12). What is that way? That we would be saved by being good—that the good people go to Heaven and the bad people go to Hell. That is what most of the world thinks. That is what most Americas think. But if you think this, you have a problem, and so do they.

What is wrong with the idea that the good people go to heaven and bad people go to hell? Let me tell you in the words of Scripture: "There is none who does good, no, not one." (Romans 3:12). Still like the idea? Where does that put all of us folks? Right in the pits! "For all have sinned and fall short of the glory of God" (Romans 3:23). Therefore, we are saved only by faith in Jesus Christ.

Why is this the case? Why is salvation by faith alone? It is in order that salvation may be of grace—by the totally unmerited favor of God—totally unearned, undeserved, unmerited, or unworked for. Salvation that is by faith in the finished work of Christ is salvation we cannot earn. Salvation by faith is salvation of grace.

Why is salvation of grace? The answer to that is, in order that it may be of God. Salvation is by faith that it may be of grace, and it is of grace that it may be of God. Benjamin Breckenridge Warfield, of Princeton, one of the greatest Greek scholars and theologians America ever produced, made this statement: "What is evangelical Christianity? Evangelical Christianity is this: That salvation from alpha to omega, from eternity to eternity, is totally of God." This is the religion that we profess.

GOD'S PROMISES—THE FOUNDATION OF OUR FAITH

Underlying all these truths—that it is of God, that it is of grace, and that it is through faith—are the promises of God. They are the written constitution upon which all else is built. "Therefore *it is* of faith that *it might be* according to grace," (Romans 4:16) . . . And whoever lives and believes in Me shall never die" (John 11:26).

Such promises are the basis for our faith and the channel for the grace of God in our lives. It could not be otherwise in a fallen world. What is the problem with a pagan religion made up of human promises? Pagan religions are always an effort on the part of man to propitiate an angry god and to reconcile himself to that god. Christianity, on the other hand, is God's successful effort to provide His own Son as an atonement to take away the penalty for sin, so that we might be reconciled unto Him.

The problem is that we simply don't keep our promises. I think of the drunk who had taken the pledge to stop drinking for the seventy-ninth time, and a friend of his, getting exasperated with the man, said, "Now, for heaven's sake, this time keep it."

He replied, "Keep it, man! I need someone to keep me!"

That is what we all need. We need someone to keep us. Our promises, as the old saying goes, are made like pie crusts— lightly and easily and quickly broken. How many promises have you broken? We talk about our politicians who give us promises and promises and more promises. "Read my lips," said one. "No more taxes—No new taxes!" What did we get? New taxes! Or how about this one—there will be a tax cut for the middle class. What did we get? The largest tax increase in history! People are wondering if politicians can keep any of the promises they make and are getting weary of them all. When I was growing up, a man's word was his bond. Today, as the cynical sign in the store said, "In God we trust. All others pay cash."

Man's word and his promises seem to mean very little. A story is told of an old California drifter who was out in the desert. Some environmentalists who were making a survey came upon him, and to their utter, abject horror, found that he had captured, killed, and eaten a giant condor—a rare and endangered species. They were so outraged, they dragged him into the city and into the courthouse and accused him of killing a member of an endangered species.

The judge was properly outraged as well, and was about to slap a harsh sentence on the man. He said, "Sir, do you have anything to say for yourself?"

"Well, judge, I was lost in the desert for a week and hadn't eaten in four days. Then all of a sudden this giant bird landed right in front of me. I just felt I had to grab it and cook it and eat it or I'd starve to death."

"I see," the judge announced. "That puts a little different light on this case. But I want to know this—if I were to let you go, would you promise to never again kill another bird that's an endangered species?"

"Oh, judge, I promise. I've never done that before and . . . and, I promise I'd never do it again."

"In that case," the judge said, "case dismissed. You may go." The drifter started to walk out of the courtroom when the judge stopped him. "I just have one question," he said. "I'm curious. What did the condor taste like?"

"Well, judge," he replied. "I would say it was sort of a cross between an American bald eagle and a spotted owl."

NOT OUR PROMISES, BUT HIS

How about our promises? "Forsaking all others, I take thee as wife (or husband) and promise—promise before God—to be faithful 'til death do us part." That is not quite as comical, is it? We are by nature promise breakers. God is *the* promise keeper, and His promises are "Yes!" and "Amen!" in Jesus Christ.

Why is it that so many church people fall backwards so often? Because their idea of growth in the Christian faith is to take a good hold on their bootstraps and pull upward. You do that and I guarantee you will find yourself flat on your back every time. The method of Christian growth in grace is not to look down at our promises, but to look up at the promises of

God and to take hold of those by faith and be lifted by God. That is the Christian method of spiritual growth—not the other way around. Thus, we see that salvation is *all* of grace.

God's promises, unlike man's promises, never fail. The Scripture says:

- God *is* not a man, that He should lie, nor a son of man, that He should repent. Has He said, and will He not do? Or has He spoken, and will He not make it good? (Numbers 23:19).

- And also the Strength of Israel will not lie nor relent. For He *is* not a man, that He should relent (1 Samuel 15:29).

- Lord, You *are* my God. I will exalt You, I will praise Your name, for You have done wonderful *things; Your* counsels of old *are* faithfulness *and* truth. (Isaiah 25:1).

- Indeed, let God be true but every man a liar. As it is written: That You may be justified in Your words, And may overcome when You are judged" (Romans 3:4).

- . . . in hope of eternal life which God, who cannot lie, promised before time began (Titus 1:2).

Truth is the substratum of all of God's character, all of His works, and all of His promises. Therefore, it is the basis of the Christian's salvation. It is the basis for the Christian's justification. It is the basis of his sanctification and growth in grace, as well.

HIS PROMISES–OUR INHERITANCE

How do we obtain these promises? We read in Scripture that in Christ all of these promises are "Yes," and in Him,

"Amen." Apart from Jesus Christ no one has any claim on any of these promises. We inherit the promises in Christ. There are thousands of specific promises in the Bible. Here are just few:

Abundant life	John 10:10
A crown of life	Revelation 2:10
A heavenly home	John 14:1-3
A new name	Isaiah 62:1-2
Answered prayer	1 John 5:14
Assurance of salvation	2 Timothy 1:12
Cleansing	John 15:3
Clothing	Zechariah 3:4
Comfort	Isaiah 51:3
Companionship [in Christ]	John 15:15
Deliverance [from sin]	2 Timothy 4:18
Divine sonship	1 John 3:1-2
Everlasting life	John 3:16
Fellowship in Jesus	Matthew 18:19
Fruitfulness	John 15:4-5
Gifts of the Spirit	1 Corinthians 12
Glory after death	Matthew 13:43
God's protecting care	1 Peter 5:6-7
Growth	Ephesians 4:11-15
Guidance	Isaiah 42:16
Hope	Hebrews 6:18-19
Inheritance	1 Peter 1:3-4
Joy	Isaiah 35:10
Knowledge	Jeremiah 24:7
Liberty	Romans 8:2
Peace	John 14:27
Power for service	John 14:12
Provision for your needs	Titus 3:5
Rest	Hebrews 4:9,11
Restoration	Isaiah 57:18
Resurrection	Romans 8:11
Rich rewards	Matthew 10:42
Spiritual fullness	John 6:35

Besides these, God has given us thousands of other promises, each one written by God. They are God's "promissory notes." Spurgeon said that God's promises are checks signed by God on the treasury of Heaven. The Bible is filled with thousands of promises. Yet many people are going around in spiritual and temporal poverty when, in fact, they have a vast treasure available to them. They are like the man who lived under a bridge and wore rags and had nothing to eat and lived a pitiful life. When he died, it was discovered that he was a long sought-for-heir who had vast millions of dollars in a bank. He never knew it, and so he never claimed it. There are many like him spiritually today, because they have never claimed the promises of God and, therefore, they are living in spiritual poverty. The question is, then, how do we obtain God's promises?

OBTAINING GOD'S PROMISES

First of all, we must find them. Suppose I took as many as a thousand checks signed by an extraordinarily wealthy person and they were made out to you, and I hid them in various places in your home—why, it would be Easter egg Sunday every day of the week. You would be searching diligently for them. Yet, that is what we have right here in His Word—these "promissory notes" from God that are contained in the Bible. So I would urge you, as you find them, to mark them in some manner in your Bible.

Second, we should learn the promises, memorize them, and hide them in our hearts. You don't want to find them and then lose them again. Hide them in your heart. You can cash them time after time after time—not just once.

Third, we need to go to God and claim each promise. If you found a check and examined and memorized what was on the check, you still wouldn't have what was promised by the check until you claimed it and went to the bank and cashed it in. We must go to Him and claim His promise: "Lord, you have promised in your Word [this or that or the other], and right now, in Jesus Christ, my Savior and Lord, by faith, I claim that promise."

Fourth, we must check and fulfill any conditions appended to the promise. For example, God makes the amazing promise in Malachi 3:10 that he will "open for you the windows of heaven and pour out for you *such* blessing that *there will* not *be room* enough *to receive it"* (Malachi 3:10). What a marvelous promise this is! But there is a condition appended to it. In the first part of that verse it says: "'Bring all the tithes into the storehouse, that there may be food in My house, and try Me now in this,' says the LORD of hosts, 'If I will not open for you the windows of heaven and pour out for you *such* blessing that *there will* not *be room* enough *to receive it.'"*

There is a condition appended to the promise. We must bring our tithes and offerings into the storehouse—then we can claim the blessing. How many people go through life barely making ends meet, worrying about money and finances, all because of unbelief—because they have not believed the promise and fulfilled the condition God has given. You can't possibly be the loser unless you ignore the promise, because He will pour out such blessings. I can tell you that He has poured blessings on me like I never would have dreamed of or believed. Thus, I have been able to continue to give more and more. He can do that for you, as well.

Finally, trust Him, for that is the last condition of obtaining the promise—believe the promise. Too often in our folly, our foolishness, and our unbelief, we act more like the ancient pagans than like modern Christians. Instead, let us search out God's promises, learn them, claim them, believe them, and enjoy seeing how God fulfills them in our lives. For this is what Christianity is all about—the God who so loved that He gave and gives again. It is about human hearts that are so touched and moved and transformed by God's love and grace, that willingly and gladly and eagerly they follow Him. For in God's school of life, in every department, in every class, on every examination, there is only one question. It appears and reappears again and again and again and again in every kind of situation, in every kind or circumstance. The question is: "Do you trust Me for this?" The evidence of growth in the spiritual life is found in trusting Him for everything—standing on the promises of God.

Chapter Eight

WHAT EVER HAPPENED TO THAT WIDOW?

You perhaps already have a good idea of what happened to that widow—God no doubt took care of her. So, too, over the centuries, God has cared for people who have trusted in Him and have demonstrated it by their giving. In this chapter, Dr. Kennedy tells the stories of a number of such individuals—stories of successful entrepreneurs who started with nothing and consistently gave the tithe, and then went on to achieve great financial success. He also tells the stories of two men whose patterns of giving set the foundations for the tremendous work they did on the mission field and in Christian ministry.

Perhaps few can match the examples of great giving described in this chapter. Nevertheless, we all can be inspired by the testimonies of their lives, and we can all aspire to trust God for all our needs— no matter what our external circumstances. Let us embrace with faith and love the promises of God set forth in this book, so that we may all find freedom from financial fear!

"So He said, 'Truly I say to you that this poor widow has put in more than all; for all these out of their abundance have put in offerings for God, but she out of her poverty put in all the livelihood that she had.'"
—*Luke 21:3-4*

What ever happened to that poor widow that we read about in this little vignette in Scripture? The passage is probably very easily passed over, but it contains within it the essential ingredient of true religion. What ever happened to that poor widow?

You know the story. Jesus, as we read in another Gospel, was in the temple sitting over against the treasury where people came and dropped in their gifts for the temple. He watched as a number of rich men dropped in large amounts of money. Then this poor widow came, and she dropped in two mites—two little coins—maybe two nickels today, and Jesus commented that she had given more than all of them had, for she had given all that she had. "For they all put in out of their abundance, but she out of her poverty put in all that she had, her whole livelihood" (Mark 12:44).

There is a lot of meat in that little phrase. Think what would happen if that were repeated today. It reminds us that an observer is watching us as well. Maybe you haven't thought about that, but every week Christ is watching as you drop in the collection plate whatever your gift is to the church. He not only knows what you gave, but from this passage we see that He knows what you kept as well. The widow gave all that she had. The others gave out of their abundance, according to Christ.

Today if a pastor were to observe what people gave and then comment on it, and if he were to commend the poor widow because she gave all that she had—he would make the newspaper. She wouldn't, but he would, because he would be accused of robbing the poor. He would be accused of taking all that this poor widow had, knowing that she did it willingly, commending her for it, and accepting it. Why, it would be scandalous! Yet Jesus did just that.

So, we may ask, what ever happened to that poor widow? How long did it take her to starve to death? Where did she sleep? What about the other basic necessities of life? She had nothing left. How you answer that question will reveal more about your true theology and religion than almost any other question that could be asked, because ultimately, the question here is, whom do we trust for all things?

THE CHOICE

This goes back to the very beginning, when Satan whispered in the ears of another woman, who was neither poor nor a widow. Satan told Eve to go ahead and eat of the fruit of the Tree of Knowledge of Good and Evil, even though God had forbidden it. He said, in effect, "God is narrow and mean and miserly. He wants your life to be miserable. But if you do it my way, you are going to be happy." She chose Satan's way—and she died.

So there is the choice. Are we going to trust in God, or are we going to trust in Satan? Generally speaking, of course, Satan doesn't reveal himself that clearly, and you are not going to see him with a pitchfork and a tail. Most of the time Satan does his work in the disguise of some very respectable person, and even more often in the disguise of you! Most people think they are doing it their way, but they are really doing it his way.

Whom do you trust in your life? Whom do you trust in when it comes to your giving? Do you trust in yourself—maybe Satan in disguise in that case—or do you trust in God? If you study the whole history of the Scriptures, you will see that God has most richly blessed those who have most fully committed themselves to Him. We can go back to the beginning of the covenant of grace with Abraham, and we'll see that God challenged him to give something more than his money. He wanted his only son. When God saw that Abraham had drawn the knife and was ready to kill his son, whom he had tied to the altar, an angel stayed his hand, for God knew that He was number one in Abraham's heart. The boy was spared, and Abraham was enormously blessed.

A MAN WHO TRUSTED COMPLETELY IN GOD

Down through the years there have been numerous others, such as Abraham, who have been greatly blessed. Maybe some of you will recall the story of Hudson Taylor, the man who opened up China to the Gospel. He was the first Christian to enter into the interior of China, a totally pagan land at that time. Before he left England, being a practical man, he began to think about how he was going to live when he got to China. There would be no mail coming from England to China. There would be no Christians there to help him. How was he going to live? What was he going to eat? Such were the practical questions of a practical missionary.

Hudson Taylor solved his problem in a way that most of us would probably never have thought of. He said, "If I am going to survive, it is going to be because God is going to provide for my needs every day." So, that night, whatever money he had, he gave away. The next day he started with nothing, and God provided his substance and his need and his food—whatever he needed that day.

At this time Taylor was going to medical school, studying to be a doctor, in order to help the people of China both physically and spiritually. At the end of each day, whatever he had more than he needed, he gave away. He began every day with zero, and he trusted in God to supply his every need. Taylor did that for days, weeks, months, years, and finally, when he left to go to China, he knew very well that God was able to supply all of his needs out of His riches in glory. Hudson Taylor was a man who trusted completely in God.

We may, therefore, know that even though that poor widow had given everything that she had, God was more than able to supply her needs. I am sure He blessed her—even abundantly.

I have a sneaking suspicion that if you heard about her again, she wouldn't be that "poor" widow who had nothing, but she would be testifying that God had blessed her abundantly!

When Hudson Taylor shared the Gospel with his brother and talked to him about serving Jesus Christ with his life, his brother said he wanted nothing to do with it. He knew what his goal in life was. He was going to be famous. He wanted fame. Fame is something that is very attractive to many people in our world today—they are living for renown, for fame. So Taylor's brother rejected the offer to accept Christ. He rejected the plea to serve Christ. He was going to be famous! Now, you all know his name—it was . . . hmm, it was . . . Hudson Taylor's brother! In every history book that mentions him, he is mentioned as "Hudson Taylor's brother"—Mr. Anonymous.

Hudson Taylor did not go to China for fame or fortune or any of those things, but God blessed him abundantly and gave him what his brother sought and never found. That, I think is an example of how God desires for us to give, so that He might bless us. Christ says, "Assuredly, I say to you there is no one who has left house or brothers or sisters or father or mother or wife or children or lands, for My sake and the gospel's, who shall not receive a hundredfold now in this time—houses and brothers and sisters and mothers and children and lands, with persecutions—and in the age to come, eternal life" (Mark 10:29-30).

BLESSINGS POURED OUT

God blesses people right here and now, as well as in the life to come. I have noticed that the more a person gives, the greater is the blessing. I have noticed this in my own life. To begin with, I noticed that when I tithed 10 percent, God provided all of my needs out of the remaining 90 percent. But it was not until I was giving the 20, 30, and 50 percent or more that the blessings *poured out.* It was then that God opened the windows of Heaven in totally unexpected ways—in ways that some of you would have difficulty believing. But I can tell you that it has been so.

This is why God asks us to bring the tithe and the offering—not in order that we might be minimized, or that our blessings might be restricted—but that He might bless us more *abundantly*. What was Satan's line? "God doesn't want you to have this because God is mean and narrow. He wants you to be poor and miserable." No! God wants to bless our lives! That is why he calls on us to give in an abundant way.

So the question is, in whom are you really trusting for the things of this world, as well as the one to come? If we do not bring our tithes and offerings to the Lord, we declare, in effect, that we are trusting in someone other than God to provide for our needs. That, of course, is very sad, because in so doing we will be missing out on many, many blessings.

LOOK AND SEE

We have an example writ large right here in the Western hemisphere. Many people don't see it, but it is almost a neon sign showing people this truth. In 1789, after this nation had been founded and George Washington had been elected president, the first thing Washington did was to bend over and kiss the Bible upon which he had taken his oath. The next thing he did was lead the members of the House and the Senate two blocks down the street for a two-hour worship service of the Triune God. During that service the nation was dedicated to God.

In that same year, in the southern part of our world, Haiti had gained freedom from its dictators. In 1804, they declared their independence from France, and committed their island to Satan and voodoo. Two hundred years later, Haiti is, I believe, the poorest country in the world. If that is not absolutely the case at this moment, it certainly has been in recent times. On the other hand, America has become the richest country in the world.

How many people have noticed what God is saying: "There

it is. Open your eyes. Look and see." See who is blessed and who is not. See who keeps His promises and who is a deceiver. See that it is Satan who is a liar from the beginning. However, God has showered His blessings upon those who trust in Him completely.

There is a beautiful poem by the English poet, Francis Thompson, "The Hound of Heaven." It describes a huge hound, the "Hound of Heaven" that is pursuing Thompson as he is fleeing through all kinds of experiences in life. This hound is threatening to devour him. Finally, he learns that that dark shadow is not a *hound*, but a *hand*. It is the hand of God, reaching out to bless him. At last it comes upon him, and with the hand, a voice saying:

All which I took from thee I did but take,
Not for thy harms.
But just that thou might'st seek it in My arms.
All which thy child's mistake
Fancies as lost, I have stored for thee at home;
Rise, clasp My hand, and come!"

God asks us to give, not to impoverish us, but that He might bless us all the more.

WHAT ABOUT TODAY?

We have seen some stories of people in past centuries that demonstrated a complete, sacrificial sense of giving, such as the poor widow and others. But what about today? Would anybody do anything like that today? You know one man that did. He started a ministry. One day his wife went away for the day. While she was gone, he called a company that gives furniture to poor people. He gave away all the furniture—the beds, chairs, and couches, the carpet, pictures on the wall—everything in the house. It was absolutely as bare as when they moved in. Then he wrote out a check to that same company for all of the money he had in the checking account.

Then his wife came home. She stepped inside the door, stopped dead in her tracks, looked around at the bare walls, the bare floors with no furniture, and immediately decided she was in the wrong apartment. She turned around, walked back out the door and looked around at the number on the apartment. Lo and behold, it was hers! She came back in and said, "What have you done? What's happened here?" He told her that he had given all of the furniture to one of those organizations that helps the poor.

She said, "You know what that means? Now we have to go out and buy all new furniture."

He said, "I don't think so. You see, I gave away all of our money too."

What ever happened to a guy like that? Well, I was in one of a number of buildings that he owns today that has $50 million worth of television equipment in it. Maybe you know that this is the story of Pat Robertson. I don't think anybody could challenge the reality of his faith. One might have said, "What ever happened to that guy?" God blessed him abundantly, and I am quite confident that God blesses all those who will trust in Him and bring their tithes and offerings to the Lord.

WILLIAM COLGATE

There's another story, not quite as recent, but just as compelling, of a young sixteen-year-old boy named Billy. He might just as well have had an empty house, because his father was without work. Finally, he told Billy something that few of us could imagine ever hearing. His father said, "Billy, you are going to have to leave because, you see, I can't afford to feed you." So young Billy put all of his worldly possessions in a bandana, put it on a pole, and walked out.

Billy didn't know how to do anything, and he didn't know where to go. He didn't know how he was going to eat. He went and sat down by the canal. There he met an old canal-boat captain, who just happened to be a Christian. Billy told this man of the terrible situation he was in. The captain said, "Well, young man, what do you know how to do?"

Billy replied, "I don't know how to do anything."

The older man said, "You must know how to do something. Didn't you ever do anything at home?"

He said, "Well, yes. My father sort of had a business on the side making candles and soap."

The canal-boat captain asked, "Well, why don't you do that? Before you do it though, let me tell you three things. One, you need to receive Jesus Christ as Lord and Savior of your life—receive the gift of everlasting life. Second, you need to learn to tithe—to give a tenth of your income. Third, you need to make an honest bar of soap."

Since Billy didn't have any other instructions of what to do with his life, he took these instructions quite seriously. He accepted Jesus Christ and the gift of eternal life, he started making soap and tithed on all that he made, and he was an honest business man. Billy grew to become "William," and William was William Colgate, as in Colgate-Palmolive. He gave a tithe. Later he gave 20 percent, 30 percent, 40 percent, 50 percent, 60 percent of his salary and more—and he used it to spread the Gospel of Jesus Christ.

JOHN D. ROCKEFELLER, SR.

Or consider another young man who was only about twelve when his father died. He didn't have anything. His mother had no support, so he went out and got a job. He made a whopping salary that first week of $1.50—this was a long time ago. He brought the coins home to his mother and dropped them in her lap. She looked at them and commended him for doing a good job at work.

Then she picked up a dime and a nickel and said, "Now here, I want you to give this to the church this week, and I want you to promise me that you will always tithe. That is called a tithe—a tenth." He tithed ever since that day until he was an old man. He said, "I've always given at least a tithe of what I have made to the Lord."

Well, little Johnny made a good bit. In fact, he became the richest man in America. In fact, at one point he was the richest man in the entire world! We know him as John D. Rockefeller, Sr., and he, too, gave a great deal of his money to advance the cause of Christ.

DR. CHARLES E. WELCH

A similar story starts with a young man and his wife who were on their way to Africa. This man was going to be a foreign missionary in Africa (My wife and I also were on our way to Africa, when we stopped off in Fort Lauderdale. We thought we were just passing through!). He and his wife arrived in New York. Before leaving for Africa, they had to take a final medical exam. His wife was found to have an unusual medical condition that prohibited her from living in the climate of Africa. What a disappointment! Then he said, "If I can't serve Him on the mission field, I will serve Him as a business man with my gifts." So he did just that. This man's father had a hobby of making unfermented wine for communion at their church. So the son took it over and began to build it up. You've probably all enjoyed some of Welch's juices at some time or other. Charles E. Welch's company prospered, and he gave a great sum of money to the work of world missions.

HENRY CROWELL

Here is a name that is probably not as familiar—Henry Crowell. As a young man in his early teens, he was told he had tuberculosis. He wasn't a Christian; he wasn't a missionary. He was just a young boy, and the doctor told him he would be dead in a year, but he also told him, "You might want to go outdoors and work. Maybe that will do you some good," for at that time there was no known cure for TB. So Henry went to work outside in the woods cutting down trees and sawing them into logs. After six or seven years had passed, he had not only gotten rid of his tuberculosis, he had developed into a very healthy, strong young man, and more importantly, he had accepted Jesus Christ as his Savior.

Now that he was healthy, Crowell wondered what he should do with his life. One day, while wandering through the woods, he came across an old, broken-down, ancient-looking building. He didn't know what it had been used for. He finally found out it was an abandoned mill that had once been used by some Quakers. He found the owner, bought the old building, started up the mill again and began to make cereal. You know it as Quaker Mills, Quaker Oats.

Crowell was called the "autocrat of the breakfast table" and sold hundreds of millions of dollars worth of breakfast cereals. He also tithed, and then he increased his giving to more than the tithe, until he was giving away vast sums of money to the work of Jesus Christ. Crowell was surprised at several things. One, it wasn't nearly as hard to tithe as he thought it was. Second, he was surprised in the very beginning how much easier it was to get by on the 90 percent than the 100. Then he was surprised how easy it was to increase the tithe from a tenth on up, which is what he continued to do.

Over centuries, over hundreds of years, people who have trusted in God, who have trusted in Christ, have demonstrated it by their giving. So when we ask, "What ever happened to that poor widow and her two mites?" Well, I don't know the details, but I am absolutely confident that God took care of her—and that abundantly!

ENDNOTES

[1] Herbert Lee Williams, *D. James Kennedy, The Man and His Ministry*. Fort Lauderdale, Florida, Coral Ridge Ministries, 1999 (special ministry edition by permission of Thomas Nelson, Inc., Publishers), pp. 267-268.

[2] The Barna Group, New Study Shows Trends in Tithing and Donating, April 14, 2008. http://www.barna.org/barna-update/article/18-congregations/41-new-study-shows-trends-in-tithing-and-donating.

[3] "Born-again Christians" are defined by the Barna Group as people who said they have made a personal commitment to Jesus Christ that is still important in their life today and who also indicated they believe that when they die they will go to Heaven because they had confessed their sins and had accepted Jesus Christ as their Savior. Respondents are not asked to describe themselves as "born again."

[4] "Evangelicals" meet the born-again criteria (see note 3) plus seven other conditions. Those include saying their faith is very important in their life today; believing they have a personal responsibility to share their religious beliefs about Christ with non-Christians; believing that Satan exists; believing that eternal salvation is possible only through grace, not works; believing that Jesus Christ lived a sinless life on earth; asserting that the Bible is accurate in all that it teaches; and describing God as the all-knowing, all-powerful, perfect deity who created the universe and still rules it today. Being classified as an evangelical is not dependent upon church attendance or the denominational affiliation of the church attended. Respondents were not asked to describe themselves as "evangelical."

[5]*Westminster Shorter Catechism.*
Q. 1. What is the chief end of man?
A. Man's chief end is to glorify God, [1] and to enjoy him forever.[2]
[1] Psalm 86, Isaiah 60:21, Romans 11:36, I Corinthian 6:20, 31, Revelation 4:11.
[2] Psalm 16:5-11, Psalm 144:15, Isaiah 12:2, Luke 2:10, Philippians 4:4, Revelation 21:3-4.